BRIAN OSEMAN was born in June 1937 in Erdington, Birmingham. He was educated at Handsworth Technical College as an electrical engineer. He eventually became an electronics designer in the weighing industry. He was a keen scout, gaining his King Scout Award, and eventually became a leader. His main hobby now is gardening and growing up to 4,000 bedding plants each year from seed.

Blood Beneath His Boots

A Story of World War Two

Blood Beneath His Boots

A Story of World War Two

Brian Oseman

ATHENA PRESS
LONDON

BLOOD BENEATH HIS BOOTS
A Story of World War Two
Copyright © Brian Oseman 2007

ISBN 10-digit: 1 84401 882 2
ISBN 13-digit: 978 1 84401 882 6

First Published 2007 by
ATHENA PRESS
Queen's House, 2 Holly Road
Twickenham TW1 4EG
United Kingdom

Printed for Athena Press

To Peggy

Peggy and Bert

Preface

My wife and I have lived next door to Peggy and Bert for the last forty-two years. I had known from the start that Bert had been a soldier in the Second World War, but it was apparent that this had been a very traumatic time for him and that he didn't want to talk about it.

Peggy began to suffer with arthritis in the joints, and about five years ago she had to have one of her knee joints replaced. This did not turn out to be successful as she contracted MRSA in the wound, so she went back into hospital to have the leg made stiff. During this period she was also complaining of stomach pains. This was not like Peggy, as she rarely complained about anything – her usual statement was 'Stop fussing, will you. I'm all right!'

The time came to go into the operating theatre, and during the operation on her knee, a duodenal ulcer burst. Although the surgeons did their very best, Peggy sadly past away while in Intensive Care the next day.

Since that very sad day, we have taken Bert under our wing, making sure he is okay.

It was during the many cups of mid-morning tea that I realised Bert had a fascinating story to tell about his time as a front line soldier during the epic struggle of World War II.

He fought all the way up the Italian peninsula and finally moved to Greece to fight the ELAS rebels.

Bert gradually found the telling of these incidents therapeutic, so a start was made at taking down the information in March 2005.

The following is a series of short descriptions of action against the enemy, amusing events, extreme terror and definable bravery.

Bert, who is now eighty-eight, cannot always remember the locations of the various incidents, so they are presented in a sequence that seemed to be appropriate.

All of the sketches/paintings are by Bert's own hand. In looking at them you should realise that he is totally colour blind and suffers from acute macular degeneration and is trying to recall happenings of sixty-two years ago.

Bert has asked me to dedicate this book to his wife, Peggy.

Hockley, Birmingham

It was a very special Christmas for the Keeling family. Alfred and Beatrice Keeling lived in Ventnor Road in the quiet suburbs of Hockley, Birmingham. It may have been very cold outside but inside there was a glow of expectation, as Beatrice was about to deliver her third child. As she already had two boys, she was quietly hoping for a little girl. However, in the early hours of Christmas morning out popped another baby boy. He was to be christened Herbert Noel, and was a brother to Ernie and Alfred. They could not have had a better present to lighten their hearts on that Christmas morning.

Bert's Dad's main profession was a jeweller, but he'd also practised some toolmaking as a fallback job. His mum, who was a full-time housewife, was a little disappointed that the baby was a boy, but I assume they were both very proud of their brand new son regardless.

It was probably a blessing in disguise, as they later lost one son, Alfred, at the early age of seven, to pneumonia. In those days this was a serious disease, which usually had fatal consequences.

The house they lived in was quite posh for the area. It had six rooms, although had no bathroom or inside toilet. It was nicely furnished, but otherwise basically equipped, and they were very proud of their Windsor armchairs. This said, it had a most important piece of furniture, a piano, in the front room. You see, in those days you made your own entertainment.

On the forthcoming winter days they would still have to troop out onto the yard to the outside facility. This would be looked on as a bit quaint in these modern times. The toilet was, of course, the usual box-and-hole affair. This was the standard in that area, and most families would have had to share with maybe as many as three other families. They were lucky, as this was their own little bit of heaven, complete with the usual sheaf of newspaper on a string. I assume the ink was not carcinogenic...

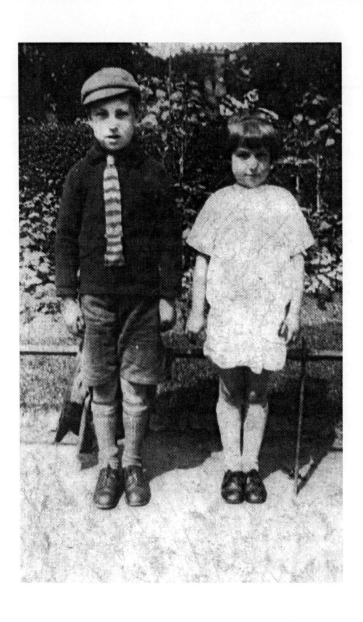

Photograph no. 1

The year was 1917, and Bert, as he is now known, grew into a nice little boy and was to be eventually presented with a little sister called Beatrice. She became a dancer and eventually a dance teacher with her husband, Charles, and is still in the same business today.

Photograph no. 1 is of Bert and his sister, Beatrice, aged nine and seven respectively. The clothes are typical of those worn at the time, and the picture was taken in Handsworth Park. In the 1920s this was a very lovely place to spend a warm summer day. This photograph would have been taken using a box camera on very slow film, which was only blue-sensitive. This meant that the definition would not be very good, as any slight movement during exposure would have caused blurring

As life progressed, Bert received the standard education in the local school, and life was very pleasant. He became friends with another boy from just along the street, Jack Pugh; they both started school at the same time.

The school was virtually at the back of the house and there were a couple of trees in the playground, one of which was still there only a few years ago - the school has, of course, long gone. He was at this same school until he reached the ripe old age of fourteen.

He left with a pass for the arts school, but unfortunately there were sixty who passed the examination, and as they were only requiring thirty pupils, Bert missed out.

He had no idea what on earth he was going to do, but one day his mum had noticed a board outside Lessor Brothers optical instrument makers, where she saw a job advertisement for a lad to make the tea... well, sort of.

They went in and made an appointment, and later that week Bert went for an interview. As you can imagine, he had just left school and had a bit of a chip on his shoulder. The boss, Harry Lessor, interviewed him for the job as a frame bender and setter.

During the interview, Bert would not call Mr Lessor 'sir'. Mr Lessor asked him if he'd called the teachers 'sir', and he said, 'Of course I did.' But he still would not say it to Harry Lessor. I don't think he really understood what was required of him. He was lucky however, as Harry did not hold this against him.

He gave Bert the job and he started his adult life, at fourteen, on the shop floor. He worked under the watchful eye of Mr Ernie Jones, who trained him in the art of bending and setting frames.

The family survived the recession of the 1930s and Bert moved up to the warehouse in the optical business. He still did the frame work but also packed the products to be sent all over the country, and did general jobs in the department. In 1938, when Bert was twenty-one, he moved into a new venture for the firm, making the spectacle frames. He didn't really want to do this but it had its advantages.

When war broke out in 1939 he was not called up for military service as he was classed as doing a reserved occupation – namely an optical technician charge hand.

His dad was a bit of a coward when the air raids started. He would run off down to the school to hide and leave his young son, Bert, to assist in fire-watching and putting out any local fires, or offering help wherever it might be needed. He used to do this watching over the top of the factory roof.

Bert was being subjected to his first contact with a thing called *War* – something that was going to affect his life in no uncertain terms. Although he did not realise it at the time, his first contact with death was to come very soon.

One night, Hockley railway station, which was at the back of Lessor Brothers, was bombed. Bert was outside on the roof as the bomb whistled over the top of the factory. Several people were killed, including the railway signalman. Tragically, his signal box had taken a direct hit and ended up as a pile of rubble. Being so close to the explosion, Bert was shaken up a bit, and he didn't move for some time. Then, when a second bomb struck the cemetery wall, the factory caretaker, Mr Partes, called him and his mate down to the cellar that doubled as a shelter and gave them a cup of tea with a tot of whisky in it.

This particular piece of bombing caused disruption to the rail traffic for some considerable time, and there was sadness for the families of those killed, especially the chap who was in the signal box; it was Bert who saw the bomb strike it.

While at Lessor Brothers, one of the workers had an internal haemorrhage while at work. The factory sent for the ambulance and after a while the management came onto the shop floor and asked for volunteers to go to the hospital with the patient to see if they could donate blood to save his life.

The hospital tested each volunteer to see if his blood matched that of the patient. If it did, they were connected via an intravenous line direct to the patient.

Unfortunately for Bert, his blood matched this fellow's group, and so he was connected to him for about thirty minutes, possibly because he was the last matching donor who had volunteered. After the donation, Bert was stretchered out of the hospital and his arm became inactive. He did not regain any use in it for at least three days after the donation.

Unfortunately the poor chap with the haemorrhage died about a week later, although every effort was made to save him. I don't think they fully understood the blood grouping requirements, or perhaps the chap was simply too ill to survive.

Moving House

Just before war was declared, Bert's father put a deposit down on a house in Rocky Lane, Great Barr, but he got cold feet when war was declared and so pulled out of the deal.

They left the rented house in Hockley and moved to different rented accommodation in the Old Oscott Lane area of the same conurbation, Birmingham. This was a poor move on his dad's part, as renting was and is, in a way, money down the drain.

Ernie had since got married and moved out to Sutton Coldfield, so this left only Mum, Dad, Beatrice and Bert in the property. It was 1941, and Bert – now twenty-four – was still doing civil defence duties and carrying out fire watches during the air raids, for the local businesses.

The move to this new property meant that Bert was no longer within walking distance of his work. This meant getting up earlier and either cycling to work or taking a bus.

Bert was a keen cyclist and would often do weekend rides all over the local area with his mates; 100-mile round trips were almost the norm. Keeping fit with weight training also took up a fair proportion of his very sparse free time.

You see, there was one other thing taking up his time these days…

Romance

Working in the same factory was a pretty young girl of sixteen whom Bert had seen before and had taken a shine too. She was called Peggy Cole, and she lived in a local back-to-back terrace block in Freeth Street, also in the Hockley area of Birmingham. Their romance slowly blossomed and soon they could not bear to be apart. Normally, work romances are renowned for being difficult, but they were smitten and it would clearly take a lot to part them. However, the world and its problems were going to have a damn good try.

Bert's love of cycling meant that he and Peggy would often go with their friends for rides out into the country.

As an example of their exploits, photograph no. 2 shows the gang out on a ride. Bert is on the left at the back, with Peggy directly in front, showing a bit of leg. Then there is Mary, Beatrice, Hilda and Dennis on the far right. Next to Peggy is Eva, the wife of the photographer. Oh yes! The photographer was Bob. They had been on a ride to Henley-in-Arden and the picture was taken on the way back at the bottom of Liveridge Hill on the Stratford road.

Bert eventually proposed to Peggy. This was a very romantic occasion, as it happened in a field just outside Knowle on the Balsall Common road. Although she accepted his proposal she was dubious about kissing him, as there were planes from Birmingham Airport flying above, and she thought she could be seen. But I'm sure she gave way in the end.

In late 1942, Bert's escape from call up faded away, as on one fateful morning the postman delivered his dreaded enlistment papers.

Photograph no.2

If anything, Bert would have liked to be in the navy, but because he suffered from extreme colour-blindness, the only choice was the army, and it was likely to be the infantry anyway. This of course now put extreme pressure on Peggy and Bert's relationship, as Peggy was now obviously very worried about what was going to happen to her one and only Bert.

Basic Training

There was a little light shining, in that he'd only been sent to a training centre in Worcester, for his six weeks of basic training. So if there was any chance of leave, it was only a thirty-mile ride away on the train.

This was Bert's first taste of army life, but being pretty fit already due to his weight training and cycling prior to the call up, he in fact enjoyed this start to this most eventful part of his life.

The square-bashing (hours of marching up and down the parade ground to instil discipline) was only one part of the training, but the other side was more serious: how to kill somebody – it started with instruction on weaponry. Being in the infantry, the rifle was going to be Bert's major weapon; so rifle training started immediately, under the name 'familiarising'.

This was carried out indoors using a P14-type rifle. This was not the normal issue weapon, as it only held five rounds of the standard 303-inch ammunition in the magazine. It was also very precise, which was another battle weapon problem. If a weapon is too precise in its firing pattern it means that you are likely to miss your target with your shot; whereas with a less accurate piece, one round spread wider might score a hit.

The weapon would be stripped down and reassembled many times and the cleaning process explained. This was done using the four-by-two rag and a pushing rod. The four-by-two was a small piece of white material 4" x 2" which fitted on the end of the rod. This cloth was then rolled around the end of the rod and inserted into the end of the barrel, having first been soaked in a small amount of gun oil. This ensured the barrel was cleaned of all propellant deposits and copper from the lining of the bullet.

After the familiarising training, the process moved outside, to where the first live firing practice was to take place. The rifle now changed to the Lee-Enfield. It was the same calibre but was not as accurate as the P14, and held ten rounds in the magazine.

The instruction started at a short range of thirty yards. The instructor let them find out the hard way that when the gun fired it was rather a fierce piece of equipment. First of all, it weighed 11 lb, and its recoil was rather potent.

Bert was very timid to start with, as this was very new territory for him, and soon found out that the rifle butt must be held hard against the shoulder to prevent bruising. Also, to achieve any accuracy, the trigger must be carefully squeezed and not jerked rapidly. It wasn't long before the process of killing people now became part of his every day training.

Bayonet training, with a straw bale representing the enemy, then followed. This helped to raise aggression and instil discipline. The idea was to run at the target with the bayonet fixed, screaming like banshee and thrusting the thing straight through the straw man.

At the end of this training Bert was transferred to the King's Shropshire Light Infantry (KSLI) for thirteen weeks of advanced training.

Now at this point Bert did something rather silly, in that he contracted acute appendicitis and was classed as critically ill. He was sent to a military hospital in Shrewsbury for urgent treatment as it was a very serious condition. His shocked family received the telegram (see plate 1) on the 1 May 1943, telling them that Bert was in hospital.

When he first went into hospital, it was decided to try and sway it away. It eased off, so he went back to the KLSI; but four weeks later he was back in hospital again to have an abscess removed. He was operated on straight away and slowly he began to recover.

Even though it was a long way for them to travel, both Peggy and Bert's mother went to the hospital from Birmingham to visit him on a regular basis.

Although at the time he did not realise it, this delay in his training meant he missed the dispatch of the other trainees to the front at Anzio. This probably saved his life. Was this the second time that Bert would dodge death?

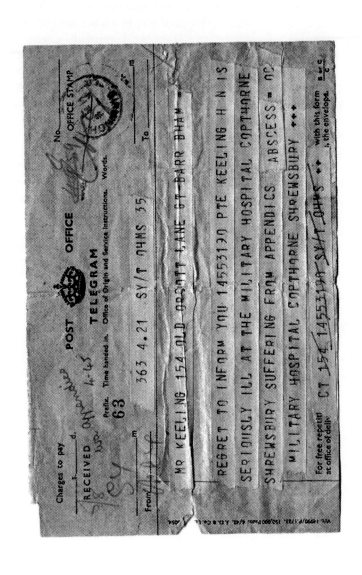

Plate 1

It was during this time that he heard that his friend from school, Jack Pugh, had been drafted into the air force as a navigator in a Blenheim bomber and had been flying over Dunkirk.

He was then moved to a convalescent home called Leighton Hall and stayed there for about two months. Peggy said he looked very smart in his blue military uniform, worn only when you are hospitalised. I think it was at this point that Peggy and Bert decided that marriage was the most important thing that they should now do, seeing that he was getting better, and would obviously be off to war very soon.

Bert did a final two-week period of recuperation at Orleton Hall, near Wellington, and at the end of this he went back to the KLSI in Shrewsbury. As Bert and Peggy had decided to get married this meant Bert had to ask for leave.

When Bert asked for leave, the officer in command at the KLSI said, 'Don't you know there's a bloody war on?' But I think this was as a joke as he eventually obtained permission for seven days' leave. This was to be six weeks in advance, so it was now all hands to the pumps to arrange the wedding.

The mammoth task of organising the wedding was taken up by Bert's mother, with Peggy doing as much as she possibly could – writing invitations, sorting out the food etc., which in itself was not an easy task what with rationing, and so on.

They were married on 18 September 1943, at St John's Church, Ladywood, with a small reception for about fifteen people, at the Farcroft public house in Handsworth. There were the parents and a few friends. Bert had swapped suits with Jack, Peggy's brother-in-law and Peggy had borrowed her sister Molly's wedding dress.

It was a very joyous occasion, with lots of singing and of course dancing, with Beatrice leading the way.

They did have a honeymoon, even though it was only for two days, to the glorious Colwyn Bay in North Wales. The journey was by train and required a change at Chester Station. They were sat in the waiting room for a long time, and opposite them was an American soldier with a young girl. Those two taught Peggy more about what she should do in the honeymoon bed than any book available…

The train to Colwyn Bay eventually arrived, and the entertainment was over for the day.

They had a fantastic time, but it was soon over and they were back in Birmingham, and Bert headed back to barracks.

Off To War

Bert was now moved to a holding battalion, in the Herefords, and then sent to Alnwick in Scotland for training in local moor sleeping. This involved being outside in a gas cape, being in a bivvy tent at night, and having only meagre rations to eat. Although this was quite tough, it was far short of what Bert was going to experience in the very near future.

He was then sent all the way down to the Isle of Wight to be stationed near Shanklin, a local seaside resort, doing coastal duty. They thought they were OK here, just strolling along the prom and watching the sea lapping on the shore. Even though it was November, they didn't mind the chill in the air; it was better than fighting.

As was typical of the army, he had only been there a few weeks when he was shipped all the way back to Greenock. On the journey back up to Scotland the train once again passed through Chester Station. This brought back strong memories of Peggy and the day they stood on the platform while waiting to move on and start their two-day honeymoon. These were to be his last days on the soil of his precious homeland for a number of years. This young man was to grow up very quickly in the next two years.

The train arrived at Greenock, pulling very slowly into the dockyard sidings. Bert now thought that up until this point, he'd control of his life, but now it would be out of his hands and down to fate. He had never been particularly religious but he felt some sort of presence in the air as the train came to a halt and all the troops had to disembark. I don't think there was any rush to get off; but Bert thought that this was it, and so he'd better just get on with it!

On Board

The docks were alive with activity. Soldiers were crammed together, with all their kit, waiting to board one of the many ships. Bert could see other vessels being loaded with munitions, vehicles and heavy guns etc. – all the paraphernalia of getting an attack force together. A lot of the force was out in the Irish Sea waiting to be loaded.

This seemed to be achieved by loading small boats with personnel and transferring them to the appropriate ship. Neither Bert nor his mates were what you would call frightened, but more intrigued as to where they might be going, and in which of these many boats they would be sailing. It turned out to be the SS *Tegelberg* (40,000 tonnes), a Dutch boat with a Javanese crew. This vessel, which used to be a luxury liner, had been converted into a troop transport ship. This meant the fitting of four pom-pom anti-aircraft weapons; there were two at the front end – I think that's the bow – and two more at the stern. The boat had a swimming pool, but this was covered over and was later used by those on board to play deck quoits, to keep the lads amused.

This boat was in fact moored against the dock. At first sight it gave the impression of being quite a large vessel. The boat looked a bit sad, but it could have been worse.

Well, it was! They were loaded almost straight away and ended up in the very bottom hold, which was six floors (or is it decks?) down. It was dark, dank, smelly and uncomfortable. In other words, it was bloody awful. There were no toilets on this deck, so it meant a climb up a narrow iron ladder to another deck for the loo.

The lads had to bring on board all the gear for future use, namely:

- Kitbag: in this was a greatcoat in khaki drill (KD); a change of underwear; denim fighting kit, and some plimsolls.

- Backpack: containing a gas cape (this was used for weather protection); a change of clothes; shaving gear; mess tins, and an enamel mug.
- Waist belt: on this belt were a jack knife and a bayonet.

The main item was of course one's weapon – it may have been a rifle, a tommy gun, or a Bren gun. Some may have had a side arm as well, in the form of a revolver. These were classed as your best friend, and had to be looked after at all costs.

The greatcoat also had pouches for ammunition, such as bullets, grenades and magazines etc.

The men carried no actual ammunition while they were on board the boat as it could have been dangerous and wouldn't be needed anyway.

They'd also been provided with what's known as khaki drill. A picture of this is shown in photograph no. 3. This set of clothes was issued for hot climates, but obviously could not be used for battle conditions. This should have given them a small clue as to their destination.

There were probably 600 men on board the *Tegelberg*, and it was good to get up on deck for a breath of fresh air. It wasn't long before the boat sailed out into the Irish Sea and anchored until the whole convoy was ready to sail. They were not told the destination; even when the final sailing orders came, and the massive fighting force set off in convoy south down the west coast of Britain.

They slept when they could in hammocks. This was probably the best, as the boat rolled about without much prompting from the sea. There was one poor soldier who was seasick for the whole journey! He had to be hospitalised on the boat to stop him becoming dehydrated. Bert felt very sorry for him.

Not much happened in the first two days, but they became familiar with the boat's various facilities. The convoy was very large and spread out over a huge area of sea. This must have been to make it more difficult for submarines to sink a lot of ships before being detected. Because of this, it was only possible, for most of the time, to see one other vessel from the top deck. Although it was not

Photograph no. 3

possible to see them, it was nice to know that the destroyers were in attendance providing protection against these hidden threats.

To break up the monotony, they did physical training on a regular basis. As you can imagine, on a boat, amongst the stores on deck, it was quite a difficult task; but it was absolutely essential to keep up the men's morale as well as their personal fitness.

By fluke, there were two men on board who were professional wrestlers. They would put on a match now and again to give the company a bit of entertainment on otherwise boring days. Other activities included the playing of bingo or housie-housie, as it was known then. There were no prizes but it passed the time. They also had other simple games. The 'tug of war' was a bit ironical given what was to come but it proved a bit of a laugh on a rolling boat. The only other important activity was, of course, boat drill.

This was the practice of getting to a particular part of the boat as fast as possible and putting on your life jacket. This jacket was supposed to keep you afloat for at least six hours. It had a light, which worked for an unknown period, but was only likely to be ten minutes or so. It also had a whistle that didn't work very well in the presence of water. It was probably best if there were no emergencies, and then you would not require it – the life jacket, of course, and not the light or whistle.

There had been no contact with the family since Bert left the Isle of Wight, and there wasn't going to be any for some time. This was obviously necessary to prevent any escape of information about where this convoy was going.

At one point in the journey the weather was extremely bad. It must be noted that it was January, and extremely cold, and to give an idea of the conditions, just off the starboard bow was the ship, the MV *Andes*. Every now and then this boat would completely disappear in the trough between waves and a few minutes later reappear again. This storm lasted for at least eight hours and affected all the personnel on board to some extent or other. The poor bloke who was sick all the time must have felt like he had already died and gone to hell!

One regular practice was the firing of the pom-pom anti-aircraft guns. The first time, Bert nearly had to go and change his trousers! These guns had quite a large calibre, about 2" in diameter, so they made an unbelievable racket with the four barrels firing in turn. This even caused the boat to vibrate violently, probably because the decks were not designed to take such weapons. These firing practice sessions only lasted perhaps a few minutes, as ammunition was valuable.

Early in the journey they were sailing past Portugal and suddenly noticed some lights on the port side. They were told by one of the gunners that this was Lisbon, and the city was of course fully illuminated, as Portugal was a neutral country. They were lucky that it was dark at the time otherwise they would have missed the show. Unfortunately, they passed through the straights of Gibraltar during the night, and so didn't really see it.

The convoy now clung to the African coast as a means of avoiding enemy ships, also the communications personnel on the boat would signal to the shore with signalling lamps. This would probably mean that radio communication was prohibited, again as a method of preventing the position of the fleet being divulged.

On one occasion panic broke out when large explosions were heard, and immediately the thought was that maybe a submarine was attacking and firing torpedoes at them. Bert was asleep at the time and did not realise that most of the soldiers were now halfway up the iron ladders heading for the top deck.

Can you imagine being in the bottom hold and being struck by a torpedo? It must have been terrifying, as you would have been below the waterline.

Suddenly a shout came down from above to say that it was, in fact, destroyers dropping depth charges. There must have been something down there, for the depth charges to be used.

The convoy carried on steaming along the African coast until it eventually arrived at the port of Alexandria. It was something like a month since they had left Britain and the Scottish port of Greenock.

A Short Break in the Desert

The weather now was totally different, even though it was February. It was fairly warm, with plenty of sunshine and a steady breeze. They did not know why they were here or how long they would be staying, but it made a change from bobbing up and down on the sea. The poor chap who was seasick was probably breathing a sigh of relief as he could now regain some of his strength. It appeared that they were not going ashore very often and when they did it was mainly for exercise.

On one of the route march outings, which there were usually around 500 men in the column, they came across an Arab woman sitting at the side of the road. She was dressed in the usual Arab clothing. That meant a garment covering her from head to foot, with a slit in it for the eyes. Amazingly, this lady was trying to offer herself to the lads for sex as they marched by, shouting to them, 'Jigger-jig, two shillings each!' or words to that effect. The mind boggles as to what she would be like, or even what you might catch. I don't think she would have received any offers, although some of the lads might have been desperate, having had no female contact for over four weeks.

Watching the action on the docks, they noticed that Arab males loaded the boats. These men, or was it boys, didn't look very old, and the word went round that they were, in fact, slaves. I am not sure that slaves existed at this time, but in that upside-down world anything was possible.

On some occasions Arabs would come to the boat and throw up oranges for the men. Unfortunately they could not eat them, as they were most likely to be contaminated, so they would have to throw them back or into the sea.

The outings usually ended up on a beach, which was about a couple of miles from the boat. It was very pleasant for them all to be able to bathe in the beautiful Mediterranean Sea, and really wash off the smelly boat from their souls. While they were at the beach an ice cream salesman arrived. He was just over the wall and attracted one or two of the lads, who went to have a look. It was at this point that something startling happened. He dropped his clothing, defecated on the roadway, readjusted his clothing and turned to the lads, offering them ice cream again. The lads who stood there were absolutely gob smacked. They turned around and walked off. I am pretty sure they wouldn't go back again for an ice cream off him, or anyone else in that area, in the near future.

Finally around 3,500 troops from the Warwickshire Yeomanry arrived from out of the desert. It was understood they were on their way back to England after having served in battle on the African mainland.

The boat now sailed for their final destination – Italy – and was loaded to the gunnels with around 4,000 souls. Thus it was a good thing that it was only going to be about three days at sea before they were due to arrive at their final destination. The journey was fairly uneventful until the last few miles.

The boat was approaching what looked like a large upturned bathtub. It could have been used for transporting refuse out to sea for dumping.

This time it was empty except for one poor bloke in the bottom. He could not get out and was shouting at the top of his voice for help. It must have been felt that, as they were so close to land, they would stop and help the poor man, as he would have undoubtedly died had he been left behind.

Well, what a performance! The method was to throw down a rope to the man. He then had to haul himself up the sixty feet to the deck on the rope. The captain must have radioed for assistance because about thirty minutes later a small boat arrived and the same rope was once again used to transfer him to the rescue craft.

Having completed its rescue mission, the boat set off again and within the hour the sight of a port brought the realisation that from now on, the state of doing nothing very much would be well and truly over.

Arrival in the Battleground: Italy

After the little diversion with the bloke in the bathtub, the boat finally steamed into the port of Taranto. It was now February 1944, and it was still nice and warm as the boat docked against what looked like a ruined castle. To say it was a bit smashed up would have been a lie. There were craters all over the place. It now became clear to the lads on the boat that it was no longer going to be a training exercise and that this was to be the real thing. The town had obviously taken a pasting; the docks were pretty well damaged and there were several ships sunk in the harbour (the Italian navy had been sunk here by the British air force earlier).

The troops who were to disembark, were taken off the boat and those who were going back to England stood on deck and wished them all luck for whatever they might encounter in the forthcoming months – and by God they were going to need it!

They were now marched to a holding area just outside the town. This march was quite an eye-opener. There were smashed buildings, great holes in the roads, and the local population looked as though they were mortified by the previous events.

They were to be in this area for about a week, and during this week they were to witness one of the most amazing sights.

On one of the exercise walks they came across a sight for sore eyes. A bomb had struck the local cemetery and had scored a direct hit in the middle of the graveyard. Most of the entombed bodies were now scattered about on the surface in a grotesque manner with the memorial stones shattered into small pieces all over the place. The centre of the cemetery was now no more than a large hole. Quite a few of the lads found this extremely disconcerting.

At one point during their week's stay at the holding camp, the other side of war raised its ugly head. All the soldiers at the camp were lined up for what they thought would be an information briefing. A senior officer came out and told the troops that a soldier had raped a local girl. As they were the only soldiers in the area at the time, it had to be one of them. He therefore had to ask if the culprit would own up.

After several minutes without any volunteers the officer had no alternative but to abandon the request, but he told them in no uncertain terms that they were 'a fucking disgusting shower!' and gave them an hour's square-bashing up and down the camp grounds. This did not make the crime any better, but no further action was taken.

The next move was further up from the port of Taranto to the Infantry Reinforcement Training Depot (IRTD). This was at the small town of San Martino, about sixty miles north. They were marched to the local sidings just outside the railway station in Taranto. I think the sidings had to be used, as the station was almost totally destroyed.

The journey was to be by train in the usual smelly cattle truck wagons. There were about 4,000 lads to load, and there were about thirty lads per wagon. This meant the train had at least 120 of these wagons hitched up to what looked like a large steam engine that had probably seen better days. The British engineers had the job of driving the train, as I don't think the Italians could be trusted, because some of them were still Nazi supporters.

This journey was to last for a mind-blowing two days of extreme discomfort. This was because the train had to stop many times for all sorts of reasons. The usual would be damaged track from previous bombing, or the engine would be running out of fuel or water, or possible enemy action; but it was slow mainly because of its extreme length. You could walk alongside just as quickly for a lot of the time.

This journey was one that at the time they thought was purgatory. They had more bruises in more places than you could imagine. I think they would have rather travelled by horse, as then they would have only been sore in one place!

There was no point in having any modesty, either, as the toilet facilities were absolutely first class. They either consisted of a bucket, or a hole in the bottom of the floor of the truck. Whenever there was a stop for some reason, the bucket would be emptied. I can only assume the contents were discarded by the trackside or maybe in a ditch. It was during these stops that most of the soldiers would jump from the train so as to use this stop to maximum effect. It was quite a sight to see a line of soldiers with their dicks hanging out piddling into a ditch.

If you had a hole in the floor, squatting down with your bum showing and the train going around a bend meant that on occasions you would miss the hole. Then of course you were landed with lousy job of having to clear up the mess. This sort of thing must have brought those on the trucks very close together as friends, which would hold them in good stead for future experiences.

The food was also up to the best restaurant standard. It only consisted of poor emergency rations. This would be 'bully beef', what we know as corned beef (only one tin to five lads.). There would also be a few biscuits and some chocolate. Now this wasn't ordinary chocolate but some dark, foul-tasting stuff, which was supposed to be a meal in one portion.

They did get tea to drink, which was served from a large Dixie-type container. So they had to scoop out a cupful, by dipping it into the ready-made mixture. It tasted a bit, no, *more* than a bit, like dishwater…

The train eventually arrived at the town of San Martino and the lads were transferred to lorries to take them to their final destination. On arrival at the IRTD the troops disembarked and were sent to their respective billets. It was at this point that Bert made one more of his dramatic moves. In getting off the lorry he accidentally sat, with some force, onto the sharp end of Joe Bowden's rifle, and it went straight up his arse and punctured his bowel.

He was in extreme pain and the tears ran down his face. Joe said that he should 'try and go for help', seeing the state he was in. He did not know where the facilities were, and thought that Bert wouldn't be able to see anyone for help until the next sick parade in the morning. He therefore suffered this extreme pain all the next night. His undergarments were soon covered in blood and on being examined the next day on parade he was sent straight to the Medical Officer (MO).

This now meant emergency treatment to rectify the problem. The MO did a good job stitching the damaged area, but this in turn meant that once again Bert was on rehabilitation, and would not be sent to the front until he was fit. The MO said, 'It was a pity the bayonet was not fixed to the rifle as it would have saved me a job.' Now there was a nice bloke.

I think that Joe was quite worried about him but he was only to see him for a short while. After about a week the rest of the lads, about 4,000, were sent on up to the monastery in the region of Cassino and to battles in and around the town of Piedmonte.

Having been left behind, Bert was sent for more training, namely a mortar firing course and finally on anti-tank training and the use of six-pounder field guns.

It was just at this point that Bert heard that his best friend, Joe, had been killed. It appeared that he had stepped onto a fragmentation mine. This was very distressing for Bert, as he knew that Joe was married with two kids.

Now these mines are lovely devices. When you tread on them, they fire a cylinder-type grenade into the air. This occurs as you step off the device, so that it flies up behind you. It contains an explosive charge and is packed with ball bearings. This explodes at about five feet in the air, inflicting obvious carnage on the person who trod on it. Bert could only take solace in the fact that Joe would have died instantaneously. This wasn't to be the first, or the last mate that Bert would be losing in the near future. Once again it seemed that Bert had escaped death due to a well timed injury. How many more times was he to unknowingly dodge the enemy's bullets?

The reason Bert found out that Joe had been killed was that some soldiers from the front had returned to the IRTD to regroup, having lost a lot of their comrades in fierce fighting. Their comment as to what it was like up at the battlefront was basically, '*Bloody hell!*' As these lads were from the 4th Division, the same as that of Bert, he could have easily have been killed too, had he not had the injury to his backside. It wasn't long before these boys were united with new members of a team and sent back up to the front.

It was during this time at the IRTD that the British and

Americans were in the process of bombing the very large monastery at Cassino. This place formed part – a big part – of World War II legend, and it was only about sixty miles to the north-west from where they were. The bombers could be heard flying overhead for long periods during the day.

Now that Bert had recovered from his injury it wasn't very long before he was ready to move up to join in the fight. The next troops to be sent were now assembled ready for departure. This time there was a big difference. They were what would be described today as 'tooled up'. It was at this point that Bert was moved to the Somerset Light Infantry Regiment which he remained in until almost the end of his time in the army.

Bert's platoon was made up of the following personnel. This may not have been all of the names and some may have been in different platoons, but it was sixty-two years ago that they were together, so to remember as many names as this is remarkable, for a man now eighty-eight years old.

Lieutenant Lane	Ginger Clewes
Corporal Caddy	Ronny Dawes
Corporal Granville	George Pope
Sergeant Jones	Slim Summerfield
Sergeant Hall	Bill Simmonds
Johnny Gibson (Gibbo)	Sticky Hughes
Duggie Renville	Titch Aldridge
Bob Fletcher	'Major' Gwyther

Now Bert had to carry, as well as his personnel kit, the following munitions:

- One phosphorous grenade
- Two type-36 grenades
- One stick grenade
- One 75 grenade. This was designed to be attached to trains or tanks using a magnet, or for demolishing walls, etc. It also requires a detonator, which was normally kept in the pouch on the uniform.

- Two Bren gun magazines
- One hundred rounds of 303 bullets
- One 18" bayonet
- A simple first aid kit (field dressing)
- One trenching tool…and on occasions a shovel.

So when I said 'tooled up' I meant it. As you can see, this kit still did not include the weapon.

While we are discussing what went to make a soldier, I think it would be a good place to describe how the army was made up during this campaign.

At the top of the tree was the corps. This corps is made up of three divisions. Then there were three brigades to each division, and there were three battalions to a brigade. Then in each battalion there were four companies, lettered A, B, C, and D, plus an 'S' unit, known surprisingly as the support unit. Now, each company had three platoons of about thirty men.

Bert's was in the 10th platoon, and was in B Company. The other platoons in this company were the 11th and 12th. Although thirty was the intended amount of men in a platoon, it was very rare for the numbers to be complete.

The battalions would be part of a regiment, say, the Somersets. There could be several battalions from different brigades in each regiment.

Each platoon would be made up of the following ratings. It must have at least one officer, usually a lieutenant; then there would be a Sergeant, two corporals and one lance Corporal. The rest of the platoon would be privates, about twenty-five if you were lucky.

Photograph no.4

The weaponry would be divided amongst the lads in the following manner: there would be two Bren guns, two tommy guns, two Piat anti-tank grenade-firing rifles, and a 2" mortar. The rest of the platoon would have the Lee-Enfield battle rifle. It should be realised that the lightest weapon would be the tommy gun at about 8 lb. So you would have to be fit to carry this entire load.

Photograph no. 4 shows four of the lads from Bert's platoon, with Bert the man at the top left. The next man on the right is someone whose name Bert cannot remember. Then there's Duggie Renville, bottom left, and Johnny Gibson – Gibbo as they all called him – bottom right.

The First Encounter with Incoming Fire

Now that they had their armoury, the situation took on a more frightening level, as they were about to set off to the front. The transport was once again by train and lorry, and the sound of the artillery grew louder as they approached the fighting. They disembarked from the lorries and were now on foot.

They had been dropped off at the rear battery of what was known as the 'Long Toms'. These were the larger field guns of about 8" calibre. They were the furthest back from the action and had a range of several miles. Hearing these firing was almost unbelievable. Don't forget this was the men's first encounter with real war.

As they made their way north they saw the monastery at Cassino. It was on their right while marching up the Liri river valley. It looked astonishing in that it stood out on top of this large hill. They could see it had been severely bombed, but they did not realise how many had died, or were yet to die, for its capture.

After walking for several hours, they came under enemy fire for the first time. This was in the form of shelling and it forced them to dodge and weave as well as jump into ditches, which they would do at the drop of hat. To say that they were scared was an understatement.

Progress was slow but they eventually came to the outskirts of the small village of Rendola. This was battalion headquarters (HQ) but the shelling was preventing them from reaching it. So at this point their progress came to a halt. The lads up front were under heavy shellfire and Bert could hear the explosions in the village and all around:

Eventually the shelling subsided, which allowed us to make further progress. When we reached the village we came across a small passageway. In the passage were a mother and daughter in extreme distress. The daughter was heavily pregnant and they were both shouting 'Inglesi! Inglesi!' at us, and holding out their hands for help. Every time a shell exploded somewhere near, the daughter started screaming and all our attempts to pacify her failed. This hurt, as we were helpless to do anything for them.

It wasn't long before some progress was made up front as the shelling began to subside, and we moved out of the passage, leaving the ladies to there own fate. This was not what we thought the first experience of dirty war would to be like, as we naively thought that only soldiers would be caught up in this degrading mess; but it was now very clear that this was not the case. It affected everyone at every level.

As they made their way out of the village they came across wounded and dead soldiers and civilians alike, but there was no way they could stop and help. They had to move on in order to reach the battalion HQ where they could take a well earned rest.

First Engagement with the Enemy

While the soldiers were at HQ they were sorted out as to which platoon they would be assigned to. This having been done, they eventually moved further north to join with soldiers already in battle. Bert was put into the 10th Platoon, which he would remain in for the rest of his time there in Italy, and the rest of his time in the army.

It turned out that the battlefront was only about one mile from HQ. This surprised Bert, as he didn't realise it was so close.

As it was to be the first engagement with the enemy for Bert, I think I should explain the typical British battle tactics at this time.

The way the fighting made progress was that an objective was determined by the senior officers at the command headquarters. This objective would have been given to a platoon. Then, having taken this objective, the platoon would hold the position while another would go through from the rear to the next objective, while this first platoon would provide covering fire if needed.

This moving forward in short distances is the well-tried technique for gaining ground without stretching the lines too far.

It was also fairly rare to actually see the enemy soldier face-to-face while using this technique. Information would come from the rear HQ that a certain location might possibly contain enemy personnel – so firing would be directed at this target.

One of Bert's first targets was a barn, so they laid down a fairly dense carpet of fire at this barn. There must have been enemy inside, as they experienced return fire.

Just a point about being on the receiving end of small arms fire. The bullets travel faster than the speed of sound and therefore produce a very loud sonic bang. The louder this bang is, the closer the bullet is to you. A little time later you may hear a dull thud; this is actually the sound of the rifle that fired it. The time between the two bangs gives an idea of the range of the firer.

If there is a fierce battle taking place you probably can't tell anything because of the extreme noise, and you'd probably be absolutely petrified anyway.

This return of fire from the barn eventually stopped, so the platoon slowly moved forward. However, when they reached it they found it empty. The enemy had retreated, so Bert's first contact with the enemy was brief and inconclusive.

Periods of Quiet

The fighting now died down for a few days and they experienced an uneasy quiet period. During these quiet periods it was possible to attend to one's physical requirements to some degree.

You could get a wash and a shave, change under clothing, and carry out the more embarrassing duties in some privacy, even if it was behind a bush or in a ditch.

Food would be provided, and if you were lucky it might even taste nice. If the action with the enemy was at a very low state and it was fairly safe, the lads would take a sleep – but only for perhaps two hours, and then it would be somebody else's turn. In some situations they would have to go without sleep for maybe two days and still come up fighting, even though they were exhausted.

The First Sight of the Enemy

The Germans once again initiated the fighting. This was firmly repulsed, but it took several days to shift them from the usual high ground they occupied. It was noticeable that the Germans were always in positions at the top of any hill in the area where the fighting was likely to be happening.

It was while taking part in this engagement that several Germans walked towards Bert waving a white flag. This was very frightening, as he wasn't quite sure how he should tackle this situation. Fortunately, next to him was a private who they called 'Major Gwyther'. He'd had a lot of experience in Africa, and was used to the surrender of an enemy.

They called him 'Major' as his stature was what you would have expected of that rank of soldier. He also had a moustache, and had a very upright way about him.

He turned to Bert and said, 'For God's sake; let them walk up to you, and in no way take your eyes off them.' You see, they had a very nasty way of looking as though they were about to surrender, and when you got close enough, several of them would step aside, allowing those behind to open up and mow you down with short-range fire.

These Germans were in fact genuine and intended to surrender, and they gave themselves up without resistance.

Bert remembers thinking that the German lads that surrendered looked no different to the lads in his platoon, and it left him wondering what all the fighting was really for.

The provost sergeant usually took any surrendering prisoners back to HQ. He would be a member of the Militarily Police, and they would effectively look after prisoners just as the normal police would at home.

Death's a Dirty Thing

The Germans were now in retreat and the lads had to march for a further fifteen miles before eventually making contact.

It is probably a good point in the story to explain what happens to the personnel who were killed in battle.

If the victim is one of your own side then the Pioneer Corps will follow up behind any attack and collect any bodies and take them back for proper burial, either in war graves, or back home for burial there.

Bert explained that there are situations when you are under fire and pinned down in one spot for several days. There may be a dead body in close proximity to your location. Now this could in fact be one of your mates, or the opposition, or even be a civilian.

After this sort of time the body will start to decay and it must therefore be buried straight away, if only to get rid of the vile smell.

Bert on several occasions had to do this. He would dig a small trench with his trenching tool and put the body into it. It would then be covered with a thin layer of soil and the person's weapon or a post stood up at the end of the grave. If the dead man had a helmet, this would be hung on the end of it to flag his presence. Once again, when they could get there, the Pioneer Corps would take the dead back to HQ for burial. It was also up to the Pioneer Corps lads to dig up the bodies that had been buried in shallow graves and return enemy dead back to the opposition or bury them in recognised war graves. This would, of course, also apply to the enemy side, who would return the bodies to Britain. What a bloody awful job!

How young is a soldier and how wicked the enemy…

The Germans had pulled back even further, and three or four days later they encountered the enemy again at a town called Ricasoli. This town was in the area of Florence.

For some reason (he can't remember why) some Italian partisans joined up with his platoon. These partisans decided to find out the German strength. They had found a local young boy who couldn't have been much more than ten years old.

They sent this little chap into the German lines to find out how many Spandau machine guns they had. He was gone for a very long time and they all thought that he must have been captured, but he suddenly reappeared and rushed over to them and said that he thought that there was about fifteen of these guns at the other end of the town. What a brave little lad!

The partisans and Bert's platoon set off to confront this force of German soldiers.

They were in a wood and when they reached the perimeter someone, shouted out towards them, in perfect English, 'Have you any wounded soldiers with you?' They were soon to find out that they were in fact German.

Sergeant Hall replied, 'Is that 12 Platoon?' Unfortunately he had made the unforgivable mistake of standing up while replying to the question and thus exposing his position to them. There was a crack of small arms fire and the sergeant fell, killed instantly.

This then started an almighty battle with Spandaus, Brens and all sorts of small arms fire. As usual, the Germans had the high ground, but it appeared that there was only a small amount of opposition.

This was again a known German ruse. They would leave a small group behind the retreating force to act as a delaying tactic, thus giving them time to move away.

The 10th Platoon only lost Sergeant Hall in this quite ferocious battle, and this was probably due to the fact that they were in a wood and quite well hidden. It was another lucky situation that saved Bert from injury.

Should the War in Italy have been ended earlier?

It was at this point that the Americans could have easily cut off the German army by going in behind them. Instead, the American General in command decided it was more important to take Rome. This was very unfortunate, as it let the German army escape in full retreat and regroup to the north.

The main bulk of the German army had now pulled back to the Albert Line just outside Florence.

A Break in Rome

There was a bit of rest and respite for the lads when they were given a trip to the recently captured Italian capital city of Rome. They stayed at the Alexander Club, which was run by the British army, and was situated just opposite the Colosseum.

As part of the trip there was a visit to a small cinema. The usherette was a young blond girl of about twenty. They could not start the film as the lads had taken out the condoms that had been issued to them and inflated them like balloons and were then tossing them into the air, I assume to try and embarrass the young lady.

Gibbo was off looking for the brothels and he had already had contact with a woman who said she could sort him out with a lady.

When he came back they obviously asked him how he got on. His reply was, 'She was a bloody grandma!' and looked very down. The lads couldn't help busting into roars of laughter at his misfortune in not getting what he had hoped for.

Unfortunately, the trip to Rome was to last only two days, so they were back on the lorries and up towards Florence to re-engage with the enemy.

Another Monastery to Take

Bert's company had made steady progress after they left the town of Terini and had now arrived at what looked like a smaller version of the monastery at Cassino. It was perched on top of a hill just like the Cassino version, so they named it 'Little Cassino' for the hell of it. It was then that they realised there was a chance that it was likely to be similar to the bigger one and so be chock-a-block with Germans.

Guess what? The orders came down that B Company had been given the task of taking it.

It was decided by someone on high, thinking of Bert, that the 11th and 12th platoons would be the first in and make a frontal attack on the monastery. This meant that Bert's 10th Platoon would be in reserve. It turned out later that the real reason the 11th and 12th platoons were picked was that they had officers available, and Bert's 10th only had a sergeant.

The attack began at night. It was quite normal to attack at night as it improved your chances of not being seen and the opposition was likely to be tired.

The 11th and 12th set off to crawl up the hill to tackle the monastery. It wasn't long before the firing started and it appeared to Bert that it was extremely intense.

The 10th set off at the rear to act as back-up. They went along a ridge, down into a valley and they eventually moved up into a small hollow, which was part of a rocky outcrop. They immediately came under intense fire and were pinned down in the hollow. The noise of the rounds passing overhead was absolutely terrifying, particularly as it was pitch dark at the time.

Sergeant Jones crawled up to a protruding rock, looked around it, and found he could see up the hill.

'Oh my God, the lads are taking a pounding!' he said, 'I think there will be a lot of casualties.'

There was one member of the platoon who was extremely

frightened; he was very timid by nature. In the middle of this battle, Gibbo picked up a small stone and threw it at this bloke and hit him on the helmet. He immediately began shouting, 'I've been hit! I've been hit!' He eventually calmed down, and did not think it at all funny, but this in fact relieved the pressure on the lads trapped in the hollow.

While the lads were trapped in this hollow, the 11th and 12th were being ripped to pieces by an overwhelming force, mainly with Spandau machine guns. It now became Bert's lads' task to provide covering fire to enable the wounded to be brought back to safety. There was a lull in the firing, which enabled Bert's platoon to get out of the hollow and make their way back down a short way to a farmhouse.

They found this place apparently empty and decided to consolidate this position as it provided a good place to give covering fire.

The wounded were slowly brought down from the battle higher up. One poor chap was brought down and the medics sat him on a wall. His legs had been riddled with bullets, but as there were men in a worse condition than him, he had to stay there until a stretcher team became available to take him down to the first aid post.

It was strange that the Germans never came down the hill to counter-attack, but maybe they thought that there was a much large force down below instead of a mere thirty men – most of whom were by now either dead or wounded.

After the firing ceased, the sergeant decided we would move into the building and take up defensive positions for the rest of the night.

As dawn broke, the Germans sent down a lot of patrols to check out the farmhouses in the area. Sergeant Jones said, 'If they come to search this farm, we fight to the finish if they find us.' That was a very sobering thought.

Sticky Hughes suddenly pipes up, 'I'll tell you what, let's cook a chicken and let some smoke out of the chimney to make them believe there are some Italians in residence.'

There were some chickens hanging up so it was possible that the place could be occupied.

Gibbo and Bert were allocated the task of guarding the passageway. While they were there they heard what sounded like jackboots coming up the steps. Bert fixed his bayonet and waited to see who would appear with some trepidation. Suddenly, out of the cellar appeared an old lady and her husband! It wasn't until Bert noticed a scarf around her head that he started to relax.

The farmer decided to go out into the field, and while he was out there some Germans and some Italian fascist soldiers came over to him and questioned him. Bert and his mates were all ready for the worst, but they eventually moved off, so the farmer obviously hadn't given them away.

Sergeant Jones, who was on guard upstairs, spotted two of these men coming down the hill. The sergeant recognised them as the fascist sympathisers who were with the Germans the farmer had spoken to.

'Right!' he said. 'You cover them from the front, and I'll go out and hide around the back of the farm, to get around behind the back of them.'

Slowly, Jones made his way around behind them. Bert and Gibson made their way towards them, arms at the ready. What a shock they had when the sergeant stuck a tommy gun into the back of one of the men! They just gave up and were captured.

Bert was now in the house with the prisoners, the owners, and about thirteen of the platoon.

Bert moved to one of the windows where Sergeant Jones was stood. They looked out and realised that there was a German soldier sitting on the ground with his back leaning against the wall while having a cigarette. The Sergeant whispered, 'If he as much as moves, he's yours.'

There was no way they were going to kill him, as the Germans had searched every other farm except theirs and to shoot him would have attracted attention. You see, I think the smoke had worked. All of the occupiers of the farmhouse were now moving about the place in their stocking feet so as not to give any sign to the soldier that they were there inside.

The soldier eventually got up and wandered off. If only he'd known how close he'd been to death…

During the following night the Sergeant decided to split the men into three groups and send them via different tracks to another farmhouse, for which he knew the reference, and knew that it should be free of the enemy. Bert's group made their way to the farmhouse via a wooded area in a valley and finally up a steep hill. It was daylight when they finally reached the rendezvous point. There were a couple of dead Germans at this farmhouse, just outside the front door. These were starting to smell so they decided to bury them with some urgency. When you're as tired as these lads were, digging graves is not high on your list of priorities, but it had to be done.

In the afternoon the sun shone on them in more ways than one. The sergeant major of C Company spotted the lads at the house and led a very tired bunch of men back to HQ where they had a well-deserved rest after such a traumatic two nights without sleep.

Death and Destruction along the Three Ridges

Bert came up with his company along the major highway, Route 9, or maybe just alongside it for safety reasons. This main road runs from Bologna up to Milan. The purpose of this long footslogging journey was to reach three ridges. The Germans were heavily defending them, and it turned out that this was to be almost their final stand on the Italian peninsular as a fighting force.

The three ridges – Coriano, San Fortunato and Vergiano – straddled the San Marino to Rimini highway. These ridges formed a German defensive position just north of the Gothic Line, which stretched virtually across Italy from the east coast to the west. It was extremely heavily defended, so the action was going to be extremely violent, as the Germans could not afford to lose. It was therefore very important that they were broken at this point.

Bert had arrived at a concentration area with the 4th Division. There were many soldiers gathered there for this offensive. The battle at the Corianna ridge had been almost continuous and going at full ferocity for about a week before Bert's division arrived.

Bert was informed that the West Kent Regiment was the first to tackle this ridge, and unfortunately had been taking a terrible pounding from a very defiant enemy.

The Black Watch had been given the job of the San Fortunato ridge, and Bert's 4th Division the Vergiano ridge.

Bert approached the ridges from the concentration area. As usual, the command had given Bert's platoon an objective. This was to be a church on the Vergiano ridge. To get to this church they would have to pass by the Coriano and San Fortunato ridges.

This first ridge had been the scene of extremely fierce fighting by the West Kent troops. Over on Bert's right, there was a Sherman tank that was burnt out, with smoke still emanating from the turret. There were three West Kent soldiers still on and in the area of the tank.

One was in the turret, one was hanging out of the door and the other was on the ground in front of it.

As far as Bert could tell, they had been trying to escape from the stricken tank but were unable to achieve this before they died from their initial injuries, were shot as they tried to get out, or just burnt to death before they made it.

In front of him there was disused canal or ditch about fifteen feet deep. Bert and the rest of the platoon had to move along this ditch to get to their destination.

On the way they came across many, many more dead. Here there was a collection of soldiers on top of each other. Some were Germans on top of some West Kents, or the other way round. There were also several individual bodies in grotesque positions, often lying in pools of blood. Further up the ditch there were another two dead soldiers lying on top of each other. It seemed odd to Bert that they should end up in this strange proximity – and that there should be so many of them. War is very difficult to comprehend, most of the time anyway.

On Bert's left there was a West Kent Bren gunner lying in the prone shooting position, still with his hands on the weapon as if he had just been firing at the enemy.

Bert could not understand why he was so still. Then he realised that the man had been shot through his head. The clue was that as he approached a little closer he could see that the poor bloke had completely lost the back of his head. The bullet had struck him in the forehead and removed the back of his skull as it passed through; an unbelievable sight.

Further on, there was another West Kent soldier who'd had his legs blown off. He was in a terrible mess, with blood all over him. He may not have died straightaway but bled to death from the horrendous wounds.

The Black Watch were tackling the San Fortunato ridge, so Bert's platoon skirted around this ridge to avoid the ongoing battle. They then came across another ditch in which the human misery became even more poignant. There was water flowing down this ditch. It wasn't much of a flow, just a gentle trickle.

The problem with it was that it was a dark red in colour.

This was coming from the bodies higher up the hill. Whether they were poor Black Watch comrades or the enemy German lads doesn't really matter. It was a lot of unnecessary dying. Bert had to cross this ditch, which meant he had to walk through the blood-filled ditch – he could physically feel the blood beneath his boots.

Bert's platoon then crossed a road, and C Company gave them covering fire to enable them to get across to the objective of the Vergiano ridge.

As explained earlier, Bert's platoon was given a church as their objective. This church was on the top of a hill, so the whole platoon got down into cover and opened up on the church with what you could possibly call withering fire at the target. As there was no return of fire, they slowly made their way up to the church, firing every now and then. This still produced no response, so it had to be assumed that there was no enemy inside. The Germans had pulled back, but when the platoon reached the church they found it was full of Italians on their hands and knees, praying.

These civilians were causing an obstruction and were a bloody nuisance. They were in the middle of the doorway and wouldn't move. One of the lads communicated with the preacher in sign language and he managed to move them to a safer position inside the church.

Just a Stray Shell

The platoon stayed there for around three days keeping watch. It was at this point that shrapnel hit Ronny Dawes. He had been outside with an Italian civilian trying to see if the enemy was about. Suddenly the shelling started up and a shell landed very close to them. A piece of shrapnel from this shell unfortunately struck Ronny in the head. He was not killed immediately but died later while being transported to the first aid post.

It appears that they found out afterwards that it was the vibration of the vehicle transporting him back to the first aid post that moved the shrapnel in his head and killed him.

It was Bert himself who ran back under shellfire to the first aid post, which was a good 300 yards back down the road, to get help for Ronny. Having reached it and got help, he then had to come back on a jeep with the driver and a stretcher to pick Ronny up. The driver then drove back with the wounded man to the first aid post, still under shellfire. They weren't to realise it at the time that it was to be of no avail. The Italian civilian who was with Ronny was also badly injured, but Bert did not know what his outcome was.

Finding a Crossing

They were eventually moved away from the church to find a way to get tanks across the Marano River. The tanks required the water to be fairly shallow with no unexpected hollows for them to get stuck in as they went across

The officer who volunteered for the task, Lieutenant Lane, made his way across a shallow part of the river dressed as an Italian peasant, while two privates, who had moved down to the edge of the river, covered him just in case he was seen by the enemy. The rest of the platoon covered these two from the church.

He made his way across, having successfully found a shallow route for the armour. When he reached the other side he continued into the woods and found no sign of the enemy. Unknown to him, the Germans had already pulled back, and that was the reason he hadn't come under fire.

He was decorated for this act of extreme bravery, which enabled tanks and heavy armour to cross the river in safety.

That Bloody Shovel!

Having secured the river, Bert's platoon eventually moved on again alongside Route 9 towards Bologna. It was dark once again, and the lads were approaching a farmhouse while walking alongside a barbed wire fence. They had just passed through an open gate to gain access to the farmhouse when there was a rumbling noise coming from the other side of the building. The lads knew immediately what it was: the dreaded sound of a Tiger tank. There was a sudden crash and the tank burst through the rear wall of the farm building. It had positioned itself inside the building and was sticking out of one end.

The lads turned around and set off at high speed back towards the gate they came through.

Bert, who was at the front of the platoon, didn't think he would make it back to the gate in time, so he dived to his right and came across the barbed wire fence. It was while tackling this wire that the Tiger tank crew opened up towards him with machine-gun fire.

It was at this point that Bert became entangled in the barbed wire. This was once again one of Bert's better moves.

What had happened was that the shovel he was carrying on his back became locked in the wire. If you can imagine it, the wire had become hooked between his back and the blade of the shovel, which was acting as a barb. This was making it impossible for him to move from his position.

The rounds from the tank were only just passing his backside. He could see the tracer rounds about two inches from his body and he was terrified.

Struggling with his predicament, Bert had to think of something fast, as he could feel the pressure of the sonic shock wave on his body.

To escape, Bert had a flash of inspiration, and decided he had to remove his backpack, which in turn would release this bloody shovel from the barbed wire.

Painting no.1

The tank was still firing, and as the rest of the platoon had pulled back, it had left Bert on his own in this frightening mess. Can you imagine trying to remove your clothing while trapped by a barbed wire fence, with a German tank firing bullets only two inches from your body?

He succeeded in removing his pack and he was now free from the barbed wire. He gathered up his bits and pieces, including that bloody shovel, and he dodged off to the left, out of the line of fire and then zigzagged to try and prevent himself from being hit.

To this day he has no idea why he wasn't hit and can only assume that the tank was at the end of the travel of the machine gun, making it impossible for them to lower the line of fire any more; so they could not hit Bert with this deadly fire.

When he eventually made his way back to the platoon, who had regrouped in a different farmhouse, the lads noticed that he was shaking like a leaf in a storm. It was the only time during any of the fighting that he thought he was going to die. He sat himself down on a grassy slope and thought a swig of Scotch would have helped. There was no chance of that out here, but it took him only about ten minutes to recover his composure.

To his surprise, the platoon was almost immediately sent back to the same place. They had to take control of the situation in this area where he had, only half an hour earlier, been entangled on the barbed wire.

Oh, what a smell! And we got forty-four this time...

They approached the enemy again, and Bert seems to remember firing at the Germans from the hip in real 'cowboy' fashion. He also remembers having to jump a cesspit. After he had success-fully cleared this, he turned around to see poor old George Pope, being very much shorter than himself, land straight in the middle of it – so you can bet he smelt lovely for the next few days, until there was a lull in the fighting and he would get chance for a change and a wash!

Sticky Hughes suddenly shouted, 'I've got some prisoners here!'

Bert couldn't believe his eyes. There were dozens of them, all very bedraggled. It took a little while, but it ended up that they had rounded up and captured forty-four of the best German paratrooper soldiers.

Bert said that just by looking at them you could tell that they had just about had enough and were glad to give up.

One of them though, had the gall to spit in Bert's face. Well, Bert too had had enough of fighting this nasty lot, so he gave the German a clonk on this shoulder with the butt of his rifle. He found out later that this bloke was an out-and-out Nazi.

Another prisoner went to put his hands into his pockets, so Bert, who was now on edge, snapped the bolt on his rifle. The poor chap shot his hands in the air and was shaking violently, fearing that Bert would shoot him.

Later on, when Bert thought about what had happened, he was a bit upset at this. You see, the chap had nothing on him; but in these situations they never knew and could not take risks.

Would you like chicken for lunch?

The 4th Division had been on the road for several days, and it was decided by Command for them to move off the road and let the 10th Indian through.

They had reached a small town called Forli, and the order came to find a billet for a few days. Bert and his mates, Gibbo, Doug Renville, Bob Fletcher and Corporal Caddy, were allocated a small bungalow, where the sole occupants were a mother and daughter.

Now, it turned out that the daughter could speak a little French, which was a little fortuitous, as so could Doug. This gave them the opportunity to settle in with some comfort.

The *casa* (Italian for a small house) was a very basic affair. There was a charcoal range used for cooking in the one and only serviceable room, and washing facilities were only a little better than that provided by the army. This was an outside well with a bucket on a rope.

This splendour therefore meant that they all had to sleep in the one room, which made the evenings interesting, to say the least. Doug was getting on very well with the daughter, and a little bit of passion seemed to be blossoming.

The lads hadn't really eaten well for some considerable time, and it came to the notice of Gibbo that down the field there was a chicken house. He rarely missed a trick! He wandered off to have a look to see if there were any chickens in it.

After a few minutes he came back to Bert and said, 'There's at least half a dozen in there… I think we should have one for dinner.'

'Whose are they?' Bert asked.

'I don't bloody know! Probably the girl's – who cares?' Gibbo replied. 'But I'm having one for dinner!'

So off he dived into the hen house to catch a bird. Then all hell broke loose and feathers were flying out of the door, as Gibbo tried to catch a hen. You'd think he was trying to get the ruddy lot!

He eventually came out of the door with a chicken, which he had firmly grasped around the neck with the head facing him. He was rotating the main body of the bird in a circular motion like the cowboys would do with a lasso, at the same time shouting at it, 'If you don't die, I'll blow your bloody head off with a grenade!'

'For Christ's sake, shut up, or you'll have the ruddy Germans down here!' Bert immediately replied.

They eventually mastered the art of breaking a chicken's neck and started the job of plucking the little blighter.

You'd think Gibbo would have known all about chickens as his dad ran a barrow in the East End of London.

They then had the brass neck to cook the bird and also share it with the ladies. They both commented on how nice it tasted, but never seemed to realise that they had in fact eaten one of their own chickens.

The Italians were very warm

At various times while marching north along the road, people would come out and great them. The young ladies would often come up to them and give them a kiss. It appears that the Germans treated them with such contempt that they were only too glad to be relieved of their burden. Earlier, just before they went into the cottage with the mother and daughter, a young girl came up to Bert and gave him a kiss and then presented him with a rosary.

He still has this to the present day, as it must have meant an awful lot to the girl for her to give it to him.

Photograph no.5

Need a bike?

While they were billeted at the little town of Forli, they went for a walk around this fascinating place. To Bert's amazement they came across a sort of cycle shop. The four of them decided that they just had to go in. Although the Italian owner could not really speak any English, sign language seemed to work wonders.

As explained earlier, Bert did an awful lot of cycling in his younger days, and to find a cycle shop in a battle-scared town, seemed remarkable.

The owner appeared to have a small stock of racing bikes, and there was one particular bike Bert had to have a good look at. This was a top of the range racer with spring wheels. To the uninitiated, this means a lightweight bike, fitted with wooden wheels; there were no high-tech alloys in those days.

These very pleasant few days with the ladies were soon over, and the Division was on the road north again. Bert said that Doug had swapped addresses with the young Italian lady, but whether they ever wrote to each other afterwards Bert has no idea.

What a dreadful mistake!

Bert's platoon had been engaging the enemy and was about to hand over the task to members of the Black Watch. The level of fighting was very intense and the Black Watch were to relieve the pressure on B Company.

The reinforcing soldiers were coming in from Bert's right and almost straight away Bert's platoon said amongst each other, 'What on earth's going on? They're walking along the ridge standing up.' Not only that, but they were outlined against the skyline.

The lads started shouting at the top of their voices, 'Get down!' But it was too late; the Germans opened up and they were cut to pieces. The lads could only watch them fall under the intense level of fire.

They were told later, via the grapevine, that the officer who led them into this position was new to the fighting and had no experience of battle conditions. It's a very hard way to find out you've done it wrong.

A Thousand Field Guns Fire

For some time there had been a build-up of Allied troops and especially artillery, where every possible piece of armament had been gathered together with the idea of a massive frontal attack on the Gothic Line. This line was, as explained before, a last stand for the German forces in Italy.

On the day of the attack, the assembled armour of at least 1000 pieces of field artillery started a creeping barrage on the Gothic Line. A creeping barrage is where the guns fire round after round at an ever-increasing range in the hope that everything in the way will be destroyed.

If the Allies were going to defeat the enemy, this would be the one and only chance to break through their lines. While the barrage was in progress the troops were on a starting line, behind the barrage, ready for the attack. During this sort of false dawn, Bert remembers his stomach was churning while they waited for the off.

The signal to move was the sounding of many whistles along the length of the line. Thinking about it, these were probably made in Bert's home town of Birmingham; but I digress.

As they set off, they realised that the ground in front of them had been ploughed to impede their advance.

How loud can you scream?

There was no resistance to their advance for some considerable distance, although it was slow going across those ploughed fields. They arrived at a ditch where there was a soldier, an Allied soldier, who was screaming at the top of his voice. Although he was not injured, he had become mentally unstable. The lads knew this as being 'bomb happy' or 'shell-shocked'.

They had to do something fairly quickly, as they were very close to the German lines, and the noise could have easily caused the enemy to find out what was going on, with disastrous results. The screaming soldier was grabbed by one of the lads further back and dragged out of the way so that the medics could look him after.

It appears that this man was part of a reconnaissance group that had been given the wrong objective. They had been walking across the path of our own artillery barrage and were extremely shaken up.

The objective they had been given was in fact Bert's objective, and this was a farmhouse about fifty yards in front of them.

Is this where Bonfire Night came from?

While advancing, they came across a whole pile of haystacks on fire. This was a sure sign that there were Germans in the area and that they should proceed with care. It was one of the Germans strategies to set fire to all the farmers' haystacks. This appeared to be because the Italians would hide their farm machinery in them to stop the Germans from destroying them. Also, the German used them to stop the advance of the Allied forces by illuminating the area.

Sure enough, they suddenly they came under fire. Bert made his way with four others towards an outhouse. There were two Bren gunners on his right and another rifleman on his left.

By the way, this was hardly an outhouse, as it had been almost completely destroyed. It may have been hit by shellfire, as there was a large hole it the back wall.

The lads were protecting themselves by using pillars or the corners of the walls for cover. It was a good job they did, because almost by surprise a German popped out from the hole and fired several bursts of machine-gun fire at them, spraying it about in a 'John Wayne' fashion. Fortunately, though, no one was actually hit.

Bert thought that there might have been other Germans behind the wall so he took the opportunity, while the German with the machine gun was reloading, to throw in a grenade. There was the usual violent explosion, and after a few seconds Bert went round the rear of the building to have a look; but the Germans had pulled back, probably expecting more of the same.

Lieutenant Toms of the 11th Platoon saw them and called them over. He seemed to be acting as their officer for the time being. Realising the situation required immediate action, he sorted them into strategic positions for the rest of the night.

On your own without a Chicken

Bert was behind what was left of the chicken house. Well, he assumes it was a chicken house; there was only a low wall remaining, and this was where Bert settled in. This time his mate, Gibbo, had been given the job of company runner, as the radio had failed, which I gather was a normal occurrence.

He had to run back and forwards with information between the officer in charge and the company command HQ that was just behind the fighting.

Bert was stuck behind the wall all night, firing at shadows that appeared in front of him; shadows that he assumed came from the light of the burning haystacks.

As Bert was firing at irregular intervals, the Germans would return fire in his general direction but they never came down to sort him out. They must have thought there were many more soldiers in front of them rather than just Bert. He explained that this was the loneliest he had ever felt in his life.

The Bren gun group was some way to his right, so this didn't help Bert with his feelings of extreme isolation.

Next morning, Lieutenant Toms, or 'Tomsie' as he was known, called Bert into the farmhouse. He pointed out some Germans, in a bit of a hollow, whom he had pinned down with a Bren gun. Bert reckons he called him back into the farmhouse to give him a break from his lonely spot, especially as the fighting was subsiding. The Germans in the hollow had eventually had enough and surrendered.

The dawn finally came, and it emerged that the shadows that Bert had been firing at were in fact counter-attacks by Germans. This showed that they had in fact come down to try and put a stop to Bert's persistent firing at what he thought were shadows.

As the daylight improved, it was apparent that there were at

Painting no.2

least ten German soldiers dead in front of were Bert was positioned; but of course Bert couldn't claim that he had killed any of them.

The surrendered soldiers had a wounded man amongst them, who had apparently been shot in the foot. The German prisoners were made to break a door off the farm building and then, as prisoners of war, made to carry him back to the first aid post using the door as a stretcher.

Where's my teeth gone?

As explained earlier, whenever possible the soldiers would use any lull in hostilities to get some rest and a bite to eat.

Bert was in the concentration area and was sitting in an 18" slit trench with a mate. Both were having a bite to eat, which he seems to remember were sandwiches. All seemed peaceful when all of a sudden a howitzer shell struck the ground about ten yards in front of them. The force of it hitting the ground caused Bert's top set of false teeth to literally fly out of his mouth while he was eating!

You would think that Bert's first priority would be to get up and see if he or anybody else was hurt, but oh no! He was after his flipping teeth and sod whether anybody was injured or not!

Once again, he was very lucky. These shells were very large calibre, and at that distance from them they should have been blown to pieces. But the shell had failed to explode; otherwise I would not be writing this book.

There appears to have been a fair amount of duff German ammunition that day, but one shell did strike a Sherman tank and completely destroy it. It was unfortunately occupied at the time, so they lost two or three more men with that one.

Who fired that one at this smelly bugger?

Bert's platoon was given the task of finding the German strength ahead of them. The platoon set off up a ditch alongside a road. They could hear the Germans talking, so they were in fact within grenade-throwing range. As they were moving by using their elbows so as not to be seen, one of the lads suddenly started to scream just like the one in the previous ditch. As they were only, say, ten yards from the enemy, the officer, Lane, threatened to shoot him. But Corporal Caddy said, 'Don't shoot him, we'll pull him out.'

He was pulled out and we all retreated after him just in case the Germans came across the road to have a look. At this point Bert noticed that he smelt like a shit house. The Germans must have been using this particular ditch as a toilet, and Bert had crawled through it! Bert was now stuck with this awful smell on his clothes for the rest of the action, however long it took…

Lieutenant Lane then decided that they should move into a canal and then into a ditch further up the road.

Bert and Gibbo were the first of the platoon to make their way up this second ditch on their bellies when suddenly Bert's shovel again caught in a wire. This time it turned out to be a signals wire that the Germans had laid along the ground between field telephones.

At this point they could hear the Germans talking again just in front of them. While in this position they were under the false impression that the rest of the platoon was still behind them. The platoon officer had, in fact, pulled the rest of the platoon back, leaving Bert and Gibbo on their own, up with the enemy.

Bert tapped on Gibbo's shoulder to tell him he was stuck, but he'd already realised what was wrong and unhooked the wire from Bert's shovel.

Corporal Caddy then came back up the trench and told them to retreat. They did this with some reluctance, and then realised that there were several Spandau positions around this trench, so if they had attacked the one at the end of the trench they would never have made it out alive.

When they had retreated a short distance, they could not resist firing a few rounds at the closest position. They then made off, as fast as their legs would carry them, back to where the platoon had regrouped.

As part of the debriefing, Colonel Chatwynd-Stapleton, known as 'Crack', requested that Bert have a chat with him on their discoveries up at the end of the ditch. They were only stood about a foot apart when a German bullet went between their faces and into the door jam in the front of a farm building.

The Colonel said, 'The cheeky bugger' and didn't even move a muscle. Bert jumped back out of the way just in case another followed it.

The Colonel was wearing his desert jacket, which was a light sandy colour and was therefore a very good target. This is what made Bert think that it was a sniper who'd fired the shot. So once again it wasn't to be his turn to die.

All gone in an instant...

Bert was coming up a hill and came across a farmer and his wife
looking down at their farm. There was some heavy shelling going
on and this German shelling had caused them to abandon their
farm in fright. Bert said that it appeared that in fact the farm was
the target. Suddenly a shell struck the farm, with a direct hit on
the main buildings.

Bert was amazed when the roof went flying into the air, the
slates fluttering down to the ground like a leaf fall in October.
The wife was on her knees, in floods of tears at seeing her home
destroyed for no real reason. Bert thought, why would the
Germans unnecessarily destroy this building? But war doesn't
seem to hold much logic with regards to what people do in the
name of what they think is right.

Is this Spain?

The platoon was holed up for the night in a cattle shed and were very pleased to have this break from the pressure of battle. They had been in the shed for about an hour when Sticky Hughes realised that there was a bull in the shed. Now, bulls aren't normally kept in with the cows, as they can get frisky when the cows come on heat.

It was at this point that Sticky decided to have a wrestling match with a bull. He grabbed the bull by the horns and was pulling and pushing it as if it was his opponent. The lads were in stitches watching this farce of a show. It was really quite dangerous, as bulls are extremely strong and injury could have ensued. Still, it did make a hilarious break in those terrible times.

Not designed as an oven

The platoon was advancing towards a ridge when they came across a Tiger tank that had been blasted by the Allies. This obviously hadn't happened very long ago, as there was still a wisp of smoke emanating from the turret. Bert decided that he would take a look inside the turret and see what was inside. Had he known what was there, I don't think he would have done it. The crew were all still in the tank. The driver and one of the crew were burnt to death. They were both still in the sitting position as though they were still driving the tank, but in fact they were unrecognisable, as they had been charred to a cinder by the intense heat within the tank.

A similar situation occurred when the platoon came across a row of Sherman tanks on a ridge. These were firing at the enemy some way off.

Bert was at the bottom of the hill watching this artillery barrage by the tanks when a German shell hit one of the Shermans. It was on fire just like the Tiger. Bert could see two of the crew jumping out from the tank with all their clothes ablaze. They rolled over and over on the grass to try and extinguish the flames, but they must have been severely burnt. Bert said that he saw no sign of any medics going to them with assistance in their hour of need.

Bert did not like the few times they were given a ride into battle on a Churchill tank. It had to be a Churchill, as this tank had a flat area for the lads to stand on. But it had one big disadvantage in that it made such a noise that they were unable to hear the sound of the incoming munitions. They were able, by experience, to estimate with some accuracy whether their name was on it. Although the tank would advance the infantry at a much greater speed, Bert still preferred to use his own legs.

Sex is ever a High Priority

Just before Faenza, Bert and Gibbo were in a farmhouse when a young girl came walking down a corridor towards them. Bert felt sorry for her as she looked in a poor state of health and he thought that she might even have had TB. They decided to offer her some of their food. She seemed very grateful, as civilians would have found obtaining food difficult. Now Gibbo, who was always on the lookout for a bit on the side, asked her if she was good for a fuck – and to Bert's surprise she actually agreed to his request.

Bert remembers being shocked by this and wondering if Gibbo was in his right mind. But he was a randy bugger, and so turned to Bert and said, 'Will you keep doggo, mate?'

In the house, the upstairs floors had collapsed and the bed in the upstairs room had fallen through leaving it at an angle between the floor and ceiling.

Never fear, Johnny and the girl moved onto this bed, while Bert moved up the corridor to keep watch for anyone who might arrive and catch them at it. After about five minutes Johnny was back, claiming it was great. Bert was a bit dubious though as she looked so ill and was not at all attractive.

A little later, the sergeant major came down the corridor, asking, 'Where is the girl that fucks?' As Bert and Gibbo had never mentioned it to anyone, they wondered if somebody else had already been with the lady before and told him about her. So they told the randy old man that they did not know where she was now; and at that, he went on his way, muttering to himself.

The news Bert had been waiting for

While they were in this farmhouse, the King's Regiment were fighting their way across the Lamone River, and had they not succeeded, Bert's Division would have had to follow them in. They always say that no news is good news, so when in the morning of the next day the command sent a messenger to say that they were being pulled out of Italy, you can imagine their reaction. This was December 1944, and it was nearly Bert's birthday, so this unbelievable news was a fantastic early birthday present. He couldn't wait to start his way back down the length of Italy to what they thought would be to Palestine for a long and well-earned rest.

Them Back Home

All the time that Bert was away from home he regularly wrote letters back to his beloved wife, Peggy, sometimes as often as one a day. These letters had to be carefully written as if they fell into enemy hands they could give valuable information on the Allied status. For this reason, every letter sent back to Blighty would be censored for this type of information. The letters in the other direction would be accumulated at the rear headquarters. When the platoons that were engaged in battle were pulled back for a rest, the mail would be handed out.

Peggy told Bert, when he eventually returned home, that she could tell when he had been in some sort of action, as there would be a gap in receiving his letters. She could hardly stand the wait until the next mail arrived and she knew he was still safe.

This situation must have been occurring to housewives, girlfriends and relations all over the world where soldiers were involved in battle.

Just a thought...

Considering all the action that Bert and the lads of the 10th
Platoon experienced, plus the fact that Hitler had used some of
his best soldiers to defend Italy, namely the Panzer Grenadiers,
the Hermann Goering Division and his top paratrooper divisions,
it is amazing that Bert was still alive. However he was, and he
thought he was now at last on his way out of the war situation.

Back on the Road

The 10th, 11th and 12th Platoons were now in a sort of euphoric state. The thought of no more fighting was more than a relief – it was a total weight of their minds and bodies.

The lads were rounded up and started their march south to the first transport back to the land of the living, rather than that of the dying.

They marched for about nine miles and reached the usual line of lorries for the journey to the railway station.

On arrival at the station, they were unusually surprised by the fact that they boarded a proper passenger train with a line of coaches. Gosh, what sumptuous luxury!

The train took them all the way to the port of Bari on the south-east coast. They disembarked from the train and were marched straight onto a boat in the dock. This was the SS *Canterbury*, which was only about half the size of the boat that had brought them here about eleven months before.

The lads were still under the impression that they were off to Palestine for a well-earned rest. Then came the shock: Palestine was out and they were told that they were off to Greece… and guess what? They were off to bloody fight again – and even worse, this was a civil war, where the enemy looked like the civilians!

Sill, they weren't there yet, so they made the most of the very pleasant journey across the Mediterranean Sea.

Arrival off the Coast of Greece

The SS *Canterbury* dropped anchor in a bay that was the approach to the port of Piraeus on the south coast of Greece. It seemed odd that they did not enter the port but they were soon to find out the reason.

After a few hours at anchor, a flotilla of small landing craft arrived at the side of the vessel. Unpleasant thoughts now entered their heads, as the idea of having to land on a defended beach was not the best of starts to a new situation.

All the boats were loaded with the soldiers and then they headed off towards the beach at the small town of Phaleron. It only took about five minutes to travel the distance from the boat to the beach. The doors at the front of the craft dropped down with a splash and then a thud. To their surprise there was not a sound: no bullets, no shells and no machine gun fire, just the gentle rippling of the waves on the sandy beach. As they walked ashore, to their amazement there was not a soul to be seen.

It appears the reason for this beach landing was that it was much easier to guarantee the safety of the soldiers on an open beach than in the confines of a port, where the possibility of rebel attack would have been very high.

At the same time as they were coming ashore, a British destroyer was shelling the outskirts of Athens, and they could hear the shells whistling overhead.

It was now December 1944, and here once again was another super birthday present for Bert. The thought of having to fight an enemy which you couldn't tell apart from the general population, was just what he had asked for!

As they moved up from the beach towards the seafront, Bert noticed that the houses built along it were very British in style. They were very stylish brick-built properties, some in very good condition.

The lads then realised that they were going to stay in one of these houses for a short while, so that the company could be sorted out ready for the task ahead.

After about two days in one of the better properties, they moved out to get to grips with the job at hand.

Who are we fighting?

In the early part of the Second World War, the British supplied the Greek partisans with arms to fight the German occupiers. It wasn't long before the Germans had had enough of Greece and decided to pull out. Some of these partisans now turned their allegiance to the Communist Party and were prodded by Russia to attempt a takeover of the Greek government. Some proof of this was the fact they received a backing from the Russians, who felt they needed a base in southern Europe and thought Greece would be a good place for it.

So there was now the silly situation where partisans, with arms supplied by Britain, had changed their name to ELAS and were fighting British soldiers, backed by Russia – who was a British ally! What a smashing situation to find yourself in!

Whose idea was the sack socks?

Bert and his mates moved off in the night to reach their more permanent headquarters.

Before they set off, they were issued with a piece of hessian sacking to place around and under their hobnailed boots, the infantry soldier's standard army issue. The idea was to keep the noise of the nails in the soles to a minimum while marching.

They set off down what was known as the 'Mad Mile' to get to a barracks belonging to the regular Greek army. The sacking was such a good idea that it fell off, or simply wore through after only a few hundred yards. Bert could not understand why they didn't wear the plimsolls, which they had in the kit, to stop the noise of the marching.

Even though they made a lot more noise than intended, they arrived safely at their destination.

This was like Home from Home…

In the grounds of the barracks there were several Sherman tanks, and to Bert's amazement there was also a full-blown NAAFI run by two young British girls. Maybe Bert was going to have the time of his life here after all!

But, oh no! On the next night they were sent out on patrol looking for any signs of the ELAS rebels.

Lo and behold, on this, their first day out, they found some of the rebels trying to blow a hole in the barracks' perimeter defences. This was a wall about ten foot thick and fifteen feet high.

Corporal Caddy decided to go back inside the barracks and warn the tank commander of what was happening rather than attacking them, as there were only five English Troops and at least twelve of the rebels.

The commander thanked the lads and said they would get the tanks ready if they came through the wall by blowing a hole in it.

After about five minutes there was a loud explosion but no hole in the wall. This meant that the rebels were unable to get through, so although the tank commander was ready he was unable to inflict any damage to their cause. When the platoon went back outside, with extra support, to where the rebels were seen setting their explosives; there was no sign of them. As you would have expected, they had evaporated into thin air once the tactic had failed. There was also very little damage to the wall, so the rebels had vastly underestimated the amount of explosive needed to really do any damage.

First Booby Trap

A few days after this incident with the wall, the company was given the objective of clearing out a street where it was known that ELAS rebels were holed up and firing from house windows at almost anything that moved. Corporal Caddy, Gibbo and Bert entered one particular property where firing had been seen emanating from earlier.

They were moving in and out of the rooms when Caddy suddenly shouted out, 'Don't touch the table!'

Bert looked at the table but couldn't understand what all the fuss was about.

Caddy turned to him and said, 'Look at the leg, Bert! Is that wire running up the edge of it?'

'Christ, yes,' said Bert. 'Is there anything underneath'?

They didn't find anything fixed there, but the explosive could have been at the other end of the wire, which went under the floor.

It was then decided to fetch in the bomb disposal boys to sort it out, as it was too difficult for them to even think of touching it. Once again, Bert missed death by just the touch of a table.

Oh my God, I nearly shot a lad!

Further on down the street they came across another house where the ELAS had been firing from various windows. Bert was undecided whether or not to throw a grenade in through the window, or put a few shots into the house. For some reason, he decided to fire through the window. Almost immediately after the rounds went into the room, a woman and a child started screaming. This was such a shock to him that against his better judgment he went into the room, not knowing what he would find – they learnt very quickly you don't trust anything or anyone. Fortunately, neither the lady nor the child, a little boy, had been hit, but Bert had to try and calm them down by saying to them the only word of Greek he knew: '*Endaxie*' – English phonetics of the Greek pronunciation – which means, 'It's all right'. The lads could not stay in this situation for very long, so they had to leave them to get back to finding the elusive ELAS rebels.

It was later back at barracks that Bert remembered the mother and daughter in the passage in the small town of Rendola in Italy, where if you remember, a similar situation occurred where a mother and daughter were screaming but they'd had to leave them to their own devices.

Method used by Rebels to avoid Capture

The command came down for the platoon to go down to some flats to investigate a report that some rebels had been firing from the windows. This seemed to be the standard routine. On the way down the patrol came under fire from the flats. Fortunately there were some tracks left by tanks that had passed through earlier, so Bert and the lads dropped into these deep ruts to avoid the fire.

The rebels stopped firing for a short while, so the platoon made a dash for the flats and fortunately managed to get into them via an open door.

When they made their way from the door into the building, with a great deal of caution, they realised that the rebels had fled – it seemed they were cowards really.

To escape quickly the rebels had blown holes in at least half a dozen of the rooms. This tactic allowed speedy movement between the rooms, thus facilitating their escape from any danger.

Nearly Shot his Mate

During the search of these flats Bert found several rooms that were locked, but he wanted to make sure that there weren't any rebels in them. So to this end he was using his rifle, just like you see in the films, to shoot the door locks off.

He had just fired at one lock when yells came from the other side of the door. Bert suddenly realised that he knew who it was, as Johnny Gibson emerged from the now open door. 'What the hell are you doing in their, Gibbo?' Bert asked with some anger, as he could have easily killed him.

'Sorry, mate, I found another way in and forgot that you were shooting the locks off.'

It turned out that the bullet had only just missed him. Another lucky escape, but if he had killed him it would have been known today as 'a friendly fire incident'. This type of thing must have happened many times during all these conflicts.

They had a laugh about it later, but as usual Gibbo was looking for something that might be worth having.

In this same block of flats they heard a noise coming from a small room. Upon investigation they found a little old man under a small sink. When they got him out he was shaking violently so Gibbo gave him a fag to settle him down. They decided to take him with them and then handed him over to the local Greek police.

It seems that whenever they went out on patrol they always had a local police officer and a Greek interpreter with them.

Sorry – wrong lot!

It was another one of those days when the platoon was on the top of a block of flats looking for any behaviour that seemed suspicious.

They had been on the roof for several hours and were just about to come down when they noticed some activity on the roof of another block of flats about 200 yards away. Bert and the lads studied the people concerned for a while and eventually decided that they were suspicious and put a few rounds in their direction. When the personnel on the other roof fired a round back at them they thought that they must have been firing at the ELAS rebels.

Now they all started firing at the roof on the other set of flats. All of a sudden, an officer of the Greek National Guard, in his posh uniform, came down the street shouting at the top of his voice, 'Stop firing, stop firing!'

Bert stopped the lad's onslaught and then asked, 'Why?'

The officer shouted back up that soldiers on the top of the other flats were also members of the National Guard – so to please stop firing!

They came down off the roof and apologised to the National Guard officer, explaining that they thought they were members of the ELAS rebels. It just shows you how dodgy this type of guerrilla warfare really was!

Are you any good at semaphore?

The platoon had been out on several occasions to places where they were certain that rebels were situated, but when they arrived they found nobody there. This had happened far too often for it to be by chance and therefore somebody must have been letting the rebels know that they were coming.

The lads were on the top of a building again, looking for the rebels who they knew had been there. Bert suddenly noticed that a woman on a rooftop opposite was hanging out washing. He then realised that it wasn't in fact wet. It then dawned on him that it was not to dry the washing, but as a signal to the rebels that the British soldiers were in the area.

Bert was off like a shot over the road and into the property. The middle-aged woman in the room had a bit of a shock when Bert arrested her and took her down to the police station for interrogation.

Another woman was in the police station when he handed her over. The officers were passing a metal detector all over the private parts of her body. Bert thought that this was a bit strange, and asked one of the officers what they were looking for. He was told it was grenades. Although it's hard to believe that a grenade could be hidden in the female genitals, women were renowned for carrying them to the rebels in this manner.

A Dreadful Day

The lads had moved out of the barracks and had settled into a block of flats closer to the action in the city. Before they set off to sort out the next load of rebels, Sticky Hughes had been swanking off one of his wartime prizes, a Luger pistol he had taken off the dead body from a German officer. This sort of thing was common practice, but they were only usually kept as mementos. For some reason Sticky decided to take it with him on this sortie. It wasn't long before they came across a gang of rebels running down the street. The rebels could see the platoon coming towards them so they smartly dodged into a cellar, which was accessed down a flight of steps. Bert thought that this was a bad move on their part, as they were now trapped in the cellar, which was under the usual block of flats.

They arrived at the flats to find that there were also civilians in residence. Sticky decided he was going to sort this lot out, and much to Bert's surprise he took out the Luger pistol. He was about ten yards away from the top of the cellar steps when there was the bang of a side arm. Sticky fell to the floor, shot through the chest. Bert had noticed Sticky take aim with the Luger, but whether he never pulled the trigger, the weapon jammed or he never cocked the piece, he'll never know. It was really stupid of Sticky to try this weapon, as he had had no training on its use, and this particular side arm is known to be prone to jamming.

Sergeant Smith now popped his head around the corner of the building to see what was happening. Immediately there was another bang and he was shot through the head, and died shortly afterwards. This was now getting out of hand, and something dramatic was needed to sort it out. Bert put down a load of fire at the top of the steps and they managed to retrieve the bodies.

After a quick discussion it was decided that perhaps the best move would be to get a tank to put a round into the cellar and sort it once and for all. A runner was sent back to rustle up a tank for the job in hand.

It was then realised that there were still some civilians in the building, so the interpreter was sent into the flats to get the locals out. There was another bang and the interpreter was also dead – shot through the chest. This was now not just a disaster, it was a tragedy, with three dead in the space of a few minutes. The local policeman managed, by shouting from outside the door, to persuade all the civilians to come outside. As explained before, whenever they went out on an operation they always had a local policeman with them.

When the tank arrived it fired a shell at short range into the cellar area and the whole dreadful scenario was over.

The remaining members of the patrol made their way back to base where there was extreme depression showing on their faces and in the hearts of these desperately sad men.

Bert had been with Sticky Hughes through the traumas of the fighting through Italy and finally into Greece – only for him to die, almost at the end of the rebels' activity in this country. It was almost too much to bear.

Nearly on a Charge

Bert, on one dark and stormy night, was given the unenviable job of sentry duty on the balcony of a set of flats. It was very dark and the wind was blowing and a metal construction was making an awful rattling noise. Bert had earlier seen the captain in and around the property, so he knew what he looked like. When the captain came past Bert later on during that dirty night, knowing who he was, Bert made the dreadful mistake of not challenging him as he approached. A simple 'Halt!' would have sufficed.

The captain came over to Bert to speak to him, but because of the wind could hardly hear what he was saying. In the end Bert realised that he was to come up before him on a charge of neglect of duty.

During the investigation, the captain studied Bert's record to date and realised that these were not his normal duties, and Bert had made the honest mistake of not challenging him, as he knew him. Also he did not want to spoil an unblemished and exemplary record, so the captain let him off with a warning.

Look what I've got!

It stuck in Bert's mind that the Greek National Guard were one of the crudest and heartless collection of so-called soldiers he had ever seen. As an example, one day a National Guard officer was coming towards Bert on a mule. It was then that Bert realised that strapped to each side of the saddle were two ELAS rebels' heads. The officer was very proud of his trophies and showed them off to everybody by riding up and down and shouting at the top of his voice.

They also had the nasty habit of killing the rebels, beheading them and sticking the heads onto the spikes of wrought iron railings. The blood would run down the iron bars and end up as a little pool under each one. If they were left there for any length of time, and they often were, the smell soon became gut-wrenching.

Look at my tree...

Bert and the lads from 10th Platoon were on the customary block of flats scouring some open land behind them for any activity by the rebels. They had been there for several hours with the usual boredom setting in. Suddenly Bert noticed a tree at the top of the field that he was almost sure was not there before. He then dismissed the idea and though it must have been there all the time and he was mistaken.

Bert happened to look at the tree about ten minutes later and it had moved a little way down the hill. Bert now decided to watch this tree more closely. Suddenly it moved a few yards further down the hill. That was it! He took aim and fired a round at the tree. It appears that all the other platoons in the area were also watching this tree, and once Bert had opened fire at the tree and the rebel behind it, about 100 rounds hit it. The noise of the firing was just like when he was pinned down in Italy. After a few minutes the firing had ceased and a small group of men came down the hill, carrying a red flag. This was to show they were medics – a bit like the Red Cross. They went over to the rebel and removed the body. By the way, they left the tree.

Bert said that he couldn't understand the mentality of the man trying this, as there wasn't another tree to be seen.

Try this for size!

Bert was in slow mode moving down one of Athens' main streets when in the distance he saw some movement in front of a house. He could see that there were several men, carrying arms, in the vicinity of the property. As he was some distance from the rebels, he decided to set the sights on his rifle to 1,000 yards and fired several shots in their direction. These bullets seemed to have no affect on the rebels and they carried on moving about in front of the house. Bert could not understand why nothing had happened, but he then realised that he was walking alongside a Sherman tank. He tapped his rifle on the side of the tank and the commander popped his head out.

He asked the commander if he could fire a couple of shells at the property. The tank had a rangefinder fitted and would be able to guarantee that the shells would strike the target. Two 2-inch rounds struck the house. After the smoke had cleared Bert had another look for movement, but there was no sign of the rebels moving about.

Bert doesn't recall whether there were any civilians in the property; but this was, after all, war, and you had to put certain things out of your mind. Bert said that he now realises why his rounds had no affect. The distance to the target was probably only 300 yards and his selection of 1,000 yards would have sent the bullets over the top of the house.

Oh my God, I've shot a child!

Bert's platoon had been sent, of all places, to the local hospital. The ELAS rebels were firing from the hospital windows and Bert said that it wasn't unusual for the rebels to use ambulances as battle wagons.

The platoon returned the fire into the windows and all went quiet. Bert then noticed that a person was entering the hospital with what looked like a box of ammunition. He therefore had no choice but to fire at the carrier, as he would have been in the hospital and the rebels would have been resupplied with munitions. Bert fired a couple of rounds in the direction of the person and he fell down onto the steps.

At this point Corporal Caddy took a look at the victim through his binoculars. He turned to Bert and said, 'I think it was a boy! I'll have another look.'

Bert's heart sank. The thought of having killed a boy was distressing. Caddy suddenly piped up again, 'The nurses have come out and have taken him in. Maybe he'll be all right'.

After about an hour without any further hostility from the hospital, the platoon decided to investigate the incident involving the young boy.

Bert became very distressed when inquiries revealed that unfortunately the lad had been fatally wounded. This misfortune still brings tears to his eyes, and it took a lot of gentle persuasion to get him to reveal the incident. Yet again this is just another sad example of what happens when humans are involved in war.

Yet another Monastery

Bert and the lads were now put on an excursion out into the hills to root out some rebels holed up in a monastery.

This place was on the top of one of those columns of rock that looked like the Old Man of Hoy off the coast of Orkney. Access to it was via a tortuous path winding its way up to the building overhanging the edge of the pillar.

As usual when they arrived at the place, the rebels had flown the nest. Having climbed all the way up the ruddy hill they weren't going to turn round again and return to base.

They found that nuns in fact occupied the building, so it was a convent. The nuns were very friendly, and the information the interpreter obtained from them was that somewhere the rebels had hidden some ammunition. This was it! The search was on, and they eventually found the store in a cave-like cellar under the rear of the building. They all stood there looking at the amount of munitions, with their mouths wide open. There were thousands of rounds of 303 bullets, mortars and grenades in boxes, but no actual weapons.

Now they had to decide what to do with it all. It couldn't be left for the rebels, should they come back. If you remember, they had to struggle up the path to get to the convent anyway. Corporal Caddy decided somebody should go back down to the village to see if they could borrow a few mules off one of the local farms.

Can you imagine the mule train making its way down the steep path loaded with enough high explosive to take half the hillside away?

The munitions were taken to a remote spot and carefully placed into a deep hollow so that they could be destroyed. It was decided that perhaps if they fired a Bren gun at the pile it would explode.

Now Caddy had to decide how far back the lads should retreat from the cash to be safe from any flying shrapnel.

With the distance carefully considered, one of the Bren gunners was set up with a magazine of tracer rounds and he let fly at the pile of ammunition. Nothing!

Caddy handed him another magazine and he had another go. Bloody hell! Talk about bonfire night – it was unbelievable! Stuff was flying in all directions and it didn't seem to want to stop.

It was so frightening that when the noise eventually stopped the lads were all still lying on the ground unable to move. After a few minutes of inaction, Caddy got up and slowly, very slowly, walked over to the hollow. There was a lot of bent metal but no actual explosive left, and the hollow was an awful lot deeper then when they first put the explosives in it.

You may well ask why they didn't use the 303 bullets for themselves. It appears that these were of Russian manufacture, and although they might well fit the weapons, how reliable would they be? In these situations the lads could not risk using possible duff stuff, so it was better destroyed.

The End of ELAS Hostilities

The news came through that the hostilities with Germany were over and that Churchill had been to Russia to discuss, among many things, the situation in Greece.

Shortly after this, Churchill came to Greece to talk to General Scobie, who was the head of the British presence in this country.

It was then that the ELAS rebels declared a truce and the hostilities ceased. It appears that Churchill had convinced Stalin not to supply the rebels with arms; so they, having lost the means of proceeding with hostilities, had given up.

Thus, over the next months of Bert's stay in this country, a change in the nature of his tasks as a soldier would occur, completely altering his role.

These tasks went from the sublime to the ridiculous – and in some cases the downright unbelievable!

Moving out of Athens

Bert hadn't realised that the wife of Sir Anthony Eden owned a large area of land to the north of Athens. On the estate was a large property which had for a short time been occupied by the ELAS rebels. They had not, as you'd say, looked after it while they were there.

It was decided that some of the British presence would be used to clean up the property, so Bert's platoon, along with others, moved into the place for a short while to carry out this clean-up.

When the lads had finished the spit and polish job on the Eden's residence, they were moved to a barn-style building on the outskirts of the town of Thebes.

As things had now settled down, the lads would be given leave to go into town as a relief from the regimented way of the army.

It was during one of these outings that a young lady was approaching them as they walked along the footpath.

Bert greeted her in Greek with the usual hello (*herete*), one of the few Greek words they knew. So when she replied back to the lads in English it was quite a shock. It turns out that she was born in Liverpool and had married a Greek ship owner.

She then invited the lads around to her house for a cup of tea and a chat, which of course they accepted with relish. From what she told them, they learned that while the Germans were in occupation she had used her house as a safe refuge for escaping British soldiers.

Then another remarkable fact emerged. It appears that her children had worked for Sir Anthony Eden's wife at the house where Bert and the boys had been clearing up only a few days before.

On another day they were again walking down the same main street of Thebes when some Greeks saw them coming. It turned out that it was the Greek National Day, and there was a meal being put on in the local town hall to celebrate. Once again the lads were invited to celebrate with them. Would you refuse a free meal after all the army food they'd had to suffer?

Prisoner of War Camp

Up in northern Greece, the platoon was given the job of guarding some German and Italian prisoners of war. As an introduction to their task they were taken on a conducted tour with one of the officers stationed there. The officer, first of all, showed them around the German quarters, and Bert realised that everything was absolutely spotless and shining bright, just as you would have expected from this meticulous race.

Now they moved onto the Italian area and, guess what, it was absolutely filthy. The Italians did have one advantage over the German. They would regularly sit on the low tin roof of the sleeping quarters and sing at the top of their voices. The sound was absolutely gorgeous with most of the interns singing in harmony. Bert, while on duty, would wander over in their direction simply to listen.

Now the camp had another strange facility, which was known as the 'shag tent'. This consisted of a fairly large marquee divided into many separate sections with canvas hanging to the floor.

This tent was used to allow the prisoners conjugal rights with their wives and girlfriends. As Bert was on guard duty at this place, it was very tempting to move the hanging canvas and see what was going on. From the noise that was often emitted, Bert reckoned that if a glass pane had been included in the design you would never have been able to see through it, as it would have been more mist than glass!

Bert wondered how the girls who had fallen for a German soldier – and there where a few – had managed to survive the ELAS rebels. As he had pointed out before, these rebels were extremely cruel, and would have beheaded the girls without a second thought if they had found them out.

Don't forget, these rebels were in fact fighting the Germans before the latter pulled out of Greece.

Always on Guard

As most of the major hostilities had now ceased, and only Japan was still on a war footing, Bert's role as a soldier changed from engaging the enemy to protecting property.

These were wide ranging, from docks, sugar factories, petrol dumps, cold storage and even brothels.

These diverse tasks were scattered all over Greece, and involved Bert in a lot of travelling. At one point he was transferred to the Regimental Police. He was not very pleased at this, as he was now separated from his platoon friends. On these various duties they would be billeted in barns, flats, houses, or even in tents.

If you've got no legs, how about a trolley?

Bert's platoon had been sent to guard a cold storage unit in the town of Patras. As was customary in these situations, the lads would get a break from guard duty and would take an excursion into town for a stroll.

They popped into a bar as soldiers normally would, and in there was a man, about twenty years old, who was stretched out on the floor. On closer examination the lads realised that the man had a sack around his legs from his waist down. It appears that he had lost his legs while fighting the Germans. Even though he had no legs he would get from the bar to the docks using only his hands.

The naval engineers who saw him regularly on the jetty decided to make his life easier and built him a seat on wheels, which he could propel with his hands. Maybe this was one of the first wheelchairs? They could see the joy on his face when he realised he was really mobile – it was a real sight to behold.

Even the Children Suffer…

Bert was back in Athens and was ordered to guard a large store of sugar. There was a little girl who would play outside the store and when the lads were on duty, she would chat away to them. This seemed to go on for ages, and even when the night fell she would still be sat there. They somehow found out where she lived, so they took her home. The parents were not the slightest bit upset and appeared not to care. In fact the children in the area were not looked after at all.

These young children were also extremely underfed and spent a lot or their time looking for food. Bert and the others who were on duty would often give them food to try and stop them diving into the swill bins outside the sugar store, looking for odds and ends.

It came to the notice of the officers that this was happening and they made the guards stop the kids from doing this rummaging.

These kids were starving as it was, and now they were banned from the only small amount of food available to them.

Bert thought this was a stupid decision, but who was he to comment? He just did what he was told.

Three Months' Leave at Last

Bert was at the town of Komotini when he received news that lifted his heart. As he had now been in a war situation for around two years he was entitled to a month's leave back in Blighty. This was to be a journey with a difference, as some of it would be in the country in which he had only just fought some of his bloodiest battles.

The first part of the journey was by boat from Greece to Italy. Then it was back on a train for the long journey to Calais, France. They went via Milan, where the train stopped in the station for a short while.

Some German soldiers, who were on the way back to their homeland, were trying to sell wooden toys that they had made while they were prisoners of war. Bert was offered one of those puppet things, which was suspended between two sticks. But as he didn't have any children he did not purchase one. Isn't it strange that one minute Bert was trying to blow the Germans to bits, and then in the next breath, he was offered handmade toys by the very same men?

The train then passed through the Alps and into Switzerland. Bert plainly remembers seeing two bridges, one below the other, and then realised that the train had just been over these two bridges that he was looking at. The train travelled on close to Interlaken and then to Basle and on into France. As Switzerland was a neutral country, it was in pristine condition with no battle scars; and because it was Switzerland everything was immaculately presented.

As the train passed into France, the surroundings once again changed back to the war-torn situation, and as they approached the coast the destruction was even worse than that which Bert had personally witnessed in Italy.

He was pleased to get off the train and get onto the boat for the trip across the Channel. The boat eventually started to move and at last he was now heading for his native land. As the white cliffs of Dover slowly came into view, a strange feeling of relief come over him. The boat docked, and after a short while he had walked down the gangplank and was on the dockside.

Bert remembers thinking how shocked he was that everyone was speaking English! Once again the damage to the fabric of the country from the years of war was obvious, but to Bert this was minor; he was on his way to spend a whole month with his brand new wife back in Birmingham.

The month sped by and Bert had to report back to the army for his return to duty. There were many tears as Bert eventually set off for the long journey back to northern Greece. It appeared that the return journey was the reverse of the outward one; the only difference was that he was now to serve in the Regimental Police, rather than as an infantryman.

Pete's Bar, and Gold-Toothed Lil

Bert had returned to Athens for a short spell of peacekeeping duty after the hostilities with the ELAS rebels had finished.

During any time off, the lads would make their way down to the town centre to one of the local entertainment establishments to relax and have a good time.

Some of these would be in the form of bars, whose sole aim was to sell drink by whatever means possible. Most of these were in the main street and had opened up almost as soon as the hostilities had ended.

Bert remembers some of the names of the bars of which the following are just a few.

The most notorious was, of course, Pete's Bar, and then there was Hyde Park Corner, Oxford Circus, and others that he can't recall. One of these, whose name he can't remember was particularly pleasant as every night it employed a girls' choir to sing popular Greek songs, and some of the lads found this extremely relaxing. Of course, there were always some members of the gathering who would still drink to excess. They'd end up having to be carried out and taken back to the billet with their arms around somebody else's shoulders, dragging their feet along the pavement and usually singing, totally out of tune, some obscene army-type song.

Now, Pete's Bar, on the other hand, was a den of iniquity. The means of getting the lads into this establishment to purchase drink was to provide sex on a grand scale. The girls who provided this sexual facility were in fact quite attractive and weren't at all scruffy in appearance but, on the other hand, they were obviously in a lifestyle fraught with terrible problems. This obviously included sexually transmitted diseases (STDs), and of course unwanted pregnancy, to name just two.

One in particular was a girl known as 'gold-toothed Lil', and yes, she did have gold fillings. She was short in stature and was no spring chicken; probably in her thirties. She was fairly hefty, with fairly large tits and a large arse. She always wore a dress and nothing much else. This enabled quick access to the necessary parts, which she would expose at the drop of a hat. On one occasion, Private Bosley, who was a regular soldier, was sat fairly close to her. She was leaning over a table talking to some American troops. (These had just been sent to Greece to help in the peacekeeping task.) She was in this position so that they could see down her front. Bosley lent over and slowly raised her frock, exposing her rear end. This revealed a totally naked rear, which he then started to stroke very gently.

For a while she didn't take a blind bit of notice, and he was taking in all the sights at the same time. Then suddenly she gave him an almighty whack, pulled down her frock and just smiled.

On regular occasions, Pete would give live exhibitions of hard core pornographic sexual activity, using Lil, or in fact any of the dozen or so girls, as his partner.

This would happen at any time when he thought that trade was dropping off. Taking hold of say Lil, he would throw her over one of the tables with her arse in the air, just in front of the lads who were drinking. Then he would lift her frock over her head so that her arse was to the wind. Without hesitation he would take out his dick and literally shove it up either her arse or her fanny, saying, 'You lads are far too slow!' and proceed to ride her for the next few minutes. As this happened the soldiers would be up on their feet, crowding around the action, shouting and screaming at the tops of their voices, 'Yes!' 'Come on!' etc.

Bert was amazed at this type of activity, but after it had happened a few times in the following weeks he became very blasé about the whole thing.

Bert often wondered how the girls protected themselves against pregnancy, as no attempt was made by Pete to use any protection, and he also made no attempt not to ejaculate into any of the girls that he demonstrated on. He had no thought for any pain they might suffer and virtually treated them as slaves to his wants.

The girls, of course, offered themselves to the customers for sexual activities of their choice. Bert found the pricing system interesting. For a particular activity, say a hand job out the back, the Greeks would pay the equivalent of sixpence, the British lads would be charged a shilling and the Americans a pound. There must have been some logic in there somewhere.

If you needed to go to the loo, it involved a trip around the back to a unisex affair, and you had no idea who would enter while you were performing. Bert said that he was in the urinal when one of the tarts entered the male area. Now this was of the usual design, featuring a steel trough at thigh level with a straight back up the wall to shoulder height, and therefore designed only for males. While Bert was piddling into the trough the tart hitched up her dress, put one foot at the top of the steel urinal, and because she was not wearing any knickers was able to also piddle into the trough at a sort of 45° angle!

Bert thought that was a funny way of getting a biology lesson, but this is Greece just after a civil war... The girl never turned a hair and just smiled through the whole affair.

Talking about urinals, on one occasion Bert went into a public convenience in the heart of the town of Salonika. As he went in he could not believe what he saw. In the middle of the room was a long table, standing in front of the table there was a line of British soldiers, all with their dicks out, dipping them into a small bowl filled with a pale blue antibacterial liquid. It was obvious that they had caught a dose of the clap – this was the consequence of having unprotected sex with ladies of ill repute!

Duties in Sierras

Bert was moved to the town of Setes, and to his surprise he was given the enviable duty of searching all the brothels in the town for the presence of British personnel. It was considered to be too risky for the lads to use these facilities due to the high risk of contracting an STD; this would of course involve a large cost to the Medical Corps for the necessary treatment etc.

These brothels fell into two distinct types. There was the state registered type, where a madam controlled the girls; and the illicit type, where the facilities were rough, to say the least, and a pimp would control the girls.

The state registered types had a row of cubicles with a girl in each. Outside these there was the madam sitting on a chair. The girls would normally be stark naked, and often came out to talk to the madam in this state without a qualm. Inside the cubicle, around the walls, were pictures of the various positions or methods that the client could choose for the sex they required. Each position came with a price alongside it – the mind boggles!

Bert's job was to go along the line of cubicles and peep inside to look for a bobbing white arse. This would have been a British soldier, and if found the man would have been arrested and taken back to headquarters, where he would have been put on a charge and may have been sent to the glasshouse for a time.

On one occasion when Bert was on duty, a Greek officer arrived and went into a special room of his own. Bert thought, gosh, he's well in to get this sort of treatment…. By some fluke, the girl didn't shut the door properly, so Bert could see inside. (Could you resist it?) He couldn't believe his eyes! The girl had taken out his tool and was gently washing it in a nice posh sink. Now, that's what he called a first-class service!

The illicit establishments were quite a different kettle of fish. If Bert was required to attend one of these, it was necessary for him to take a revolver and a pickaxe handle with him. He remembers one particularly frightening incident. The place was down a long flight of steps with a high wall on each side. If anything had gone wrong, he would have stood no chance of defending himself. But duty was duty, and he actually came across two blokes from the British contingent in this establishment. He arrested them and they were taken back to the guardroom and put on a charge. They were eventually found guilty and sent to the glasshouse with hard labour for about twelve months.

The Boat Docked and the Girls Got On

A merchant ship came into dock and the captain commandeered all the prostitutes from the town onto the ship for pleasure of the crew. This caused uproar in the town, as the usual customers were now deprived of their sexual diversion.

Bert was on dockyard duty and every now and then a used French letter would land by him on the quayside. It is surprising that one never landed on his head, so he moved from walking along the birth edge to dodge this unexpected shower.

The merchant seaman where in the town the next night and were visiting the usual bars. The girls were playing the lads up, and one was rubbing her naked bottom up and down the groin area of one of the blokes when he suddenly shouted, 'Oh, my God – I've shot my load!'

This type of behaviour seemed to be the norm in this post-conflict country.

This was it! Going Home for Good…

Bert was on another of his guard duty jobs at the town of Kavala in the north of the country. It had been the usual dull day of walking up and down waiting for something to happen. Then he saw his commanding officer walking over to him. He remembers thinking, 'Oh, blimey, what have I done now?

After a few words with the officer, Bert realised that he was about to be demobbed.

The next day, Bert was on a train to the port of Piraeus to join a boat for the start of his final journey out of the army and back to ordinary life as a civilian.

This time the boat sailed to a town near to the city of Toulouse in southern France. After disembarkation, Bert then went by train to the port of Calais. Once on the boat, Bert realised that he would not be going back in the opposite direction again.

Back in Britain, Bert had to travel to Aldershot to be properly released from his epic two years in the Army as a front line soldier. He was given his demob suit etc., a payment of £75, and a train ticket to Birmingham.

Bert got off the train and made his way to the house in Balsall Heath, where his wife had been waiting and praying for his safe return.

In 1954, Bert purchased a property in Sutton Coldfield. Then in 1963, I purchased the property next door. We have been very close neighbours all of this time, and after his wife died two years ago, he became dependant on us for his shopping and his transport etc. Considering he is now eighty-eight years old, his zest for life is just amazing – and may it continue for many years to come.

Photograph no. 6 shows the medals presented to Bert at the end of his service as a soldier. From left to right are the King Shropshire Light Infantry cap badge, the 1939 to 1945 Star, the Italian Campaign Medal, the Victory Medal and finally the Somerset Regimental cap badge

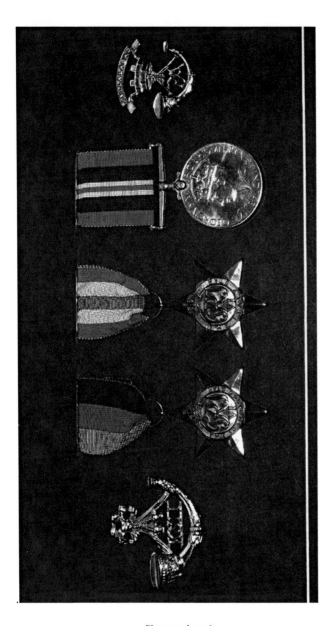

Photograph no.6

Lightning Source UK Ltd.
Milton Keynes UK
24 November 2009

146640UK00001B/21/A

9 781844 018826